M000119734

CRACKING THE

SUCCESS

CODE 2ND EDITION

ISBN: 978-1-7369881-4-5
LCCN: 2021922393

Most CelebrityPress® titles are available at special quantity discounts for bulk purchases for sales promotions, premiums, fundraising, and educational use. Special versions or book excerpts can also be created to fit specific needs.

For more information, please write:
CelebrityPress®
3415 W. Lake Mary Blvd. #9550370
Lake Mary, FL 32746
or call 1.877.261.4930

Visit us online at: www.CelebrityPressPublishing.com

CRACKING THE

SUCCESS

CODE 2ND EDITION

CelebrityPress®
Lake Mary, Florida

CONTENTS

CHAPTER 1

THE POWER OF CHARISMA

BY BRIAN TRACY

Webster's Ninth New Collegiate Dictionary defines charisma as "a personal magic of leadership arousing special popular loyalty or enthusiasm for a public figure."

Charisma is also that special quality of magnetism that each person has and that each person uses to a certain degree. You have a special charisma to the people who look up to you, who respect and admire you—the members of your family and your friends and coworkers. Whenever and wherever a person feels a positive emotion towards another, he imbues that person with charisma, or attractiveness.

In trying to explain charisma, some people speak of an "aura." This aura is a light that is invisible to most people, but not to everyone, and that radiates out from a person and affects the people around that person in a positive or negative way. The halo around the heads of saints and mystics in many religious paintings was the artist's attempt to depict the light that people reported seeing around the heads of these men and women when they were speaking or praying, or in an intense emotional state.

You also have an aura around you that most people cannot see but that is there, nevertheless. This aura affects the way people react and respond to you, either positively or negatively. There is a lot that you can do, and a lot of good reasons for you to do it, to control this aura and make it work in your best interests.

If you're in sales, this aura, reflecting your level of charisma, can have a major impact on the way your prospects and customers treat you and deal with you. Top salespeople seem to be far more successful than the average salespeople in getting along with their customers. They're always more welcome, more positively received and more trusted than the others. They sell more, and they sell more easily. They make a better living, and they build better lives. Salespeople with charisma get far more pleasure out of their work and suffer far less from stress and rejection. The charismatic salesperson is almost invariably a top performer in his field and enjoys all the rewards that go with superior sales.

If you're in business, developing greater charisma can help you tremendously in working with your staff, your suppliers, your bankers, your customers and everyone else upon whom you depend for your success. People seem naturally drawn to those who possess charisma. They want to help them and support them. When you have charisma, people will open doors for you and bring you opportunities that otherwise would not have been available to you.

In your personal relationships, the quality of charisma can make your life more joyous, and happier. People will naturally want to be around you. Members of your family and your friends will be far happier in your company, and you will have a greater influence on them, causing them to feel better about themselves and to do better at the important things in their lives.

There is a close association between personal charisma and success in life. Probably 85 percent of your success and happiness will come from your relationships and interactions with others. The more positively others respond to you, the easier it will be for you to get the things you want.

In essence, when we discuss charisma, we are talking about the law of attraction. This law has been stated in many different ways down through the centuries, but it basically says that you inevitably attract into your life the people and circumstances that harmonize with your dominant thoughts.

In a sense, you are a *living magnet*, and you are constantly radiating thought waves, like a radio station radiates sound waves, that are picked up by other people. Your thoughts, intensified by your emotions, as radio waves are intensified by electric impulses, go out from you and are picked up by anyone who is tuned in to a similar wavelength. You then attract into your life people, ideas, opportunities, resources, circumstances and anything else that is consistent with your dominant frame of mind.

The law of attraction also explains how you can build up your levels of charisma so that you can have a greater and more positive impact on the people whose cooperation, support and affection you desire.

The critical thing to remember about charisma is that it is largely based on *perception*. It is based on what people think about you. It is not so much reality as it is what people perceive the reality of you to be. For example, one person can create charisma in another person by speaking in glowing terms about that person to a third party. If you believe that you are about to meet an outstanding and important person, that person will tend to have charisma for you at first sight.

One of the most charismatic people in the world was Mother Teresa of Calcutta. In a physical sense, she was a quiet, elderly, frail woman in poor health, and she wore a modest nun's habit. She might have been ignored by a person passing her on the street, were it not for the tremendous charisma she had developed and for the fact that her appearance was so well-known to so many people as a result.

If someone told you that he was going to introduce you to a brilliant, young self-made millionaire who was quiet and unassuming about his success, you would almost naturally imbue that person with charisma, and in his presence, you would act quite differently than you would if you had been told nothing at all. Charisma begins largely in the mind of the beholder.

Of course, lasting charisma depends more upon the person you really are than upon just the things you do. Nevertheless, you can build the perception of charisma for yourself by utilizing the ten great powers of personality that seem to have a major impact on the way that people think and feel about you.

The first of these powers is the power of *purpose*. Men and women with charisma and personal magnetism almost invariably have a clear vision of who they are, of where they're going and of what they're trying to achieve. Leaders in sales and management have a vision of what they're trying to create and why they're doing what they're doing. They're focused on accomplishing some great purpose. They're decisive about every aspect of their lives. They know exactly what they want and what they have to do to get it. They plan their work and work their plan.

In more than 3,300 studies of leadership, in every book and article ever written on leadership, the quality of purpose, or vision, was one of the few qualities that was consistently used in describing leaders.

You can increase your charisma and the magnetism of your personality by setting clear goals for yourself, making plans to achieve them, and working on your plans with discipline and determination every day. The whole world seems to move aside for the person who knows exactly where he is going. In fact, the clearer you are about your purposes and goals, the more likely people will be to attribute other positive qualities to you. They will see you, or perceive you, as being a better and more admirable human being. And when you have clear goals, you begin attracting to yourself the people and opportunities necessary to make those goals a reality.

The second personality power is *self-confidence*. Men and women with charisma have an intense belief in themselves and in what they are doing. They are usually calm, cool and composed about themselves and their work. Your level of self-confidence is often demonstrated in your courage, your willingness to do whatever is necessary to achieve a purpose that you believe in.

People are naturally attracted to those who exude a sense of selfconfidence, those who have an unshakable belief in their ability to rise above circumstances to attain their goals.

One of the ways you demonstrate self-confidence is by assuming that people naturally like you and accept you and want to do business with you. For example, one of the most powerful ways to close a sale is simply to assume that the prospect has decided to purchase the product or service, and then go on to wrap up the details. One of the best ways to achieve success in your relationships is to assume that people naturally enjoy your company and want to be around you, and then proceed on that basis. The very act of behaving in a self-confident manner will generate personal charisma in the eyes of others.

The third power you can develop is *enthusiasm*. The more excited you are about accomplishing something that is important to you, the more excited others will be about helping you to do it. The fact is that emotions are contagious. The more passion you have for your life and your activities, the more charisma you will possess, and the more cooperation you will gain from others. Every great man or woman has been totally committed to a noble cause and, as a result, has attracted the support and encouragement of others—in many cases, thousands or millions of others.

The fourth personality power that you can develop is *expertise* or competence. The more knowledgeable you are perceived to be in your field, the more charisma you will have among those who respect and admire that knowledge because of the impact it can have on their lives. This is also the power of excellence, of being recognized by others as an outstanding performer in your field. Men and women who do their jobs extremely well and who are recognized for the quality of their work are those who naturally attract the help and support of others. They have charisma.

The fifth power of personality that gives you charisma in the eyes of others is thorough *preparation* prior to undertaking any significant task. Whether you are calling on a prospect, meeting with your boss, giving a public talk or making any other kind of presentation, when you are well prepared, it becomes clear to everyone. The careers of many young people are put onto the fast track as a result of their coming to an important meeting after having done all their homework.

Whether it takes you hours or even days, if an upcoming meeting or interaction is important, take the time to get on top of your subject. Be so thoroughly prepared that nothing can faze you. Think through and consider every possibility and every ramification. Often, this effort to be fully prepared will do more to generate the respect of others than anything else you can do.

Remember that the power is always on the side of the person who has done the most preparation and has the best notes. Everything counts. Leave nothing to chance. When you do something related to your work or career, take the time to do it right—in advance.

The sixth power that gives you charisma is *self-reliance*, or selfresponsibility. The most successful men and women are intensely selfreliant. They look to themselves for the answers to their questions and problems. They never complain, and they never explain. They take complete ownership of projects. They volunteer for duties and step forward and accept accountability when things go wrong.

An amazing facet of human nature is that when you behave in a completely self-reliant manner, others will often be eager to help you achieve your goals. But if you seem to need the help and support of others, people will avoid you or do everything possible not to get involved with you.

One of the most admirable qualities of leaders, which lends a person charisma in the perception of others, is the capacity to step forward and take charge. The leader accepts complete responsibility for getting the job done, without making excuses and blaming anyone. When you become completely self-reliant, you experience a tremendous sense of control and power that enhances your feeling of well being and that generates the charisma that is so important to you in attracting the help of others.

The seventh personality power is *image*. There is both interpersonal image and intrapersonal image. Intrapersonal image, or self-image, is the way you see yourself and think about yourself in any situation. This selfimage has an inordinate impact on the way you perform and on the way others see you and think about you. Your self-image plays an important part in your charisma.

The other type of image is interpersonal. This is the image or appearance that you convey to others. The way you look on the outside has an inordinate impact on the way people treat you and respond to you. Successful men and women are very aware of how they are coming across to others. They take a good deal of time to think through every aspect of their external appearance to assure that it is helping them rather than hurting them.

Remember that *everything counts*. If an element of your image is not building your charisma and your respect in the eyes of another person, it is probably lowering your charisma and your respect. Nothing is neutral. Everything is taken into the equation. Everything counts.

The three primary factors in personal appearance are clothes, grooming and accessories. Select your clothes with care. Before you go to an important meeting, stand in front of the mirror and ask yourself, "Do I look like one of the best people in my field?" If you don't feel that you look like one of the best people in your business, go back to the closet and change.

Look at the most successful people in your area of endeavor. What do they wear? How do they dress? How do they wear their hair? What kind of accessories do they use? Pattern yourself after the winners in your field, the people who already have personal magnetism and charisma. If you do what they do, over and over, you will eventually get the same results that they get.

The eighth form of personal power is *character*, or integrity. Men and women who possess the kind of charisma that arouses the enthusiastic support of others are invariably men and women with high values and principles. They are extremely realistic and honest with themselves and others. They have very clear ideals, and they continually aspire to live up to the highest that is in them. They speak well of people, and they guard their conversation, knowing that everything that they say is being remembered and recorded. They are aware that everything they do is contributing to the formation of their perception by others. Everything about their character is adding to or detracting from their level of charisma.

When you think of the most important men and women of any time, you think of men and women who aspired to greatness and who had high values for themselves and high expectations of others. When you make the decision to act consistent with the highest principles that you know, you begin to develop charisma. You begin to become the kind of person others admire and respect and want to emulate. You begin to attract into your life the help and support and encouragement of the kind of people you admire. You activate the law of attraction in the very best way.

The ninth power of personality is *self-discipline*, or self-mastery. Men and women of charisma are highly controlled. They have a tremendous sense of inner calm and outer resolve. They are well organized, and they demonstrate willpower and determination in everything they do.

The very act of being well organized, of having clear objectives and of having set clear priorities on your activities before beginning, gives you a sense of discipline and control. It causes people to respect and admire you. When you then exert your self-discipline by persisting in the face of difficulties, your charisma rating goes up.

Men and women who achieve leadership positions, who develop the perception of charisma in others, are invariably those who possess indomitable willpower and the ability to persist in a good cause until success is achieved. The more you persist when the going gets rough, the more self-discipline and resolve you develop, and the more charisma you tend to have.

The tenth power that you can develop, which underlies all of the other powers that lead to charisma, is *result-orientation*. In the final analysis, people ascribe charisma to those men and women who they feel can most enable them to achieve important goals or objectives.

We develop great perceptions of those men and women we can count on to help us achieve what is important to us. Men and women who make big sales develop charisma in the minds and hearts of their coworkers and superiors. They are spoken about in the most positive way. Men and women who are responsible for companies or departments that achieve high levels of profitability also develop charisma. They develop what is called the "halo effect." They are perceived by others to be extraordinary men and women who are capable of great things. Their shortcomings are often overlooked, while their strong points are overemphasized. They become charismatic.

Charisma actually comes from working on yourself. It comes from liking and accepting yourself unconditionally as you do and say the specific things that develop within you a powerful, charismatic personality.

When you set clear goals and become determined and purposeful, backing those goals with unshakable self-confidence, you develop charisma. When you are enthusiastic and excited about what you are doing, when you are totally committed to achieving something worthwhile, you radiate charisma. When you take the time to study and become an expert at what you do, and then prepare thoroughly for any opportunity to use your knowledge, skill or experience, the perception that others have of you goes straight up.

When you take complete responsibility and accept ownership, without making excuses or blaming others, you experience a sense of control that leads to the personal power that is the foundation of charisma. When you look like a winner in every respect, when you have the kind of external image that others admire, you build your charisma. When you develop your character by setting high standards and then disciplining yourself to live consistent with the highest principles you know, you become the kind of person who is admired and respected everywhere. You become the kind of person who radiates charisma to others. Finally, when you concentrate your energies on achieving the results that you have been hired to accomplish, the results that others expect of you, you develop the reputation for performance and achievement that inevitably leads to the perception of charisma.

You can develop the kind of charisma that opens doors for you by going to work on yourself, consistently and persistently, and becoming the kind of person everyone can admire and look up to. That's what charisma is all about.

About Brian

Brian Tracy is one of the top business experts and trainers in the world. He has taught more than 5,000,000 salespeople in 80 countries.

Brian is the President of Brian Tracy International, committed to teaching ambitious individuals how to rapidly increase their sales and personal incomes.

For more information on Brian Tracy programs, go to:
• www.briantracy.com

CHAPTER 2

OWN YOUR STORY & GIVE POWER TO YOUR VOICE THROUGH PUBLIC SPEAKING

BY DR. CHERYL WOOD

I remember it like it was yesterday... September 18, 2010 was my first time going to the front of the room to step on stage to speak. I was preparing to serve as a featured speaker for a women's entrepreneur conference hosted by Morgan State University in Baltimore, Maryland. When I arrived at the venue, my heart was racing, my palms were sweating, and my stomach was in knots. As the time approached for me to take the stage, I began feeling more and more unqualified for this speaking opportunity. And that feeling only grew as I looked at the event program and began reading the bios of the other speakers. Their bios made me sink deeper into the belief that each of them was so much more qualified than me. I started to question whether saying yes to this opportunity was a big mistake. "Cheryl, what were you thinking when you said yes?" I asked myself. "What makes you think you're an expert? The other speakers are way more qualified than you! Do you really think the women in this audience want to hear what you have to say?"

Although I briefly became sidetracked by my self-limiting thoughts, I quickly shifted my focus to the task at hand. Before I knew it, I looked at my watch and realized it was finally my time. My mind was all over the place. I wondered, "Are they going to like me? Will my words come out right? Are they going to know this is my first time speaking? Am I going to sound smart enough?" To my surprise, all the nervousness, fear, and anxiety I was experiencing was accompanied by a level of unexpected excitement and enthusiasm about the possibility that I just might say *something* that would inspire or encourage someone in the room.

Finally, the facilitator introduced me, "Our next speaker coming to the stage is Cheryl Wood," and read my bio. I held the microphone tightly, took a deep breath, smiled brightly, and began with the opening statement of my speech. As I continued to speak, I was shocked! The words I wanted to express were flowing freely as if I had years of experience in public speaking. I wasn't looking at my notes. I wasn't questioning whether or not I was good enough. Instead, I felt energized, excited, and honored to share my knowledge.

Midway into my speech, an even greater shift happened within me when I looked around the room to observe the audience's reaction to my delivery. Some were taking copious notes, others were nodding their heads in agreement, and some attendees had tears in their eyes as they listened to my story and my 'big why'. Afterwards, the feedback from the attendees was soul-stirring. The women shared their big takeaways, asked robust follow-up questions, boldly spoke up about their commitment to press through their own fears and self-limiting beliefs, and set goals for taking action towards achieving their own dreams. The icing on the cake was hearing attendees say, "You were talking directly to me... I needed to hear this message today!" Those words filled my soul and created a sense of internal fulfillment that I had never experienced before.

From that day on, I knew I wanted to experience that type of fulfillment for the rest of my life. More importantly, I knew I wanted to make other people feel empowered and inspired like that for the rest of my life. A fire was lit within me, and a passion for helping others was ignited. As my coach Les Brown often says, I was "hungry" to explore how I could use my story and the power of my words to fuel hope, belief, passion, inspiration, information, and empowerment into women globally.

On that day, I realized both my story and my voice were indeed the formula for *Cracking the Success Code*. As time went on, the more I shared my story and gave power to my voice, the more lives I impacted. This became the catalyst for making my unique fingerprint felt in the world, creating a living legacy, and building my million-dollar speaking and coaching business. I learned the power of not discounting my knowledge or devaluing the impact of my story. I became more comfortable coming to the front of the room to speak publicly, even when it felt scary. Soon I was no longer focusing on being qualified to speak, but rather I knew that I had been *called and equipped* to share my voice.

The great news is that you also have been *called and equipped* to share your voice through public speaking! Being *called and equipped* isn't based on a long list of qualifiers. Rather, it signifies that there is something inside of you that's craving to speak up and share your experiences, successes, triumphs, and failures with others to remind them that they're not alone. It signifies that you are passionate and prepared to share ideas, advice, and strategies to help others persevere, overcome, and bounce back from challenges and obstacles because you've "been there, done that" and can offer viable solutions. However, being *called and equipped* does not negate the urgency of developing the skill of public speaking and mastering the art of effective verbal communication so that you can make the greatest impact.

So, if you've been feeling a yearning in your spirit to share your story and give power to your voice, but you've been quietly staying in the background, I challenge you to come out of hiding and boldly speak on stages to share what you know. Remember, *"Somebody is waiting on what you're sitting on."* Now is the time to turn up the volume on your voice!

When I made the decision to own my story and give power to my voice through public speaking, I started by implementing the five steps below. These steps will serve you well also:

1. Validate for yourself that your story matters, that it carries weight, and contains a unique, transformative message. Avoid the tendency to seek external validation to convince you that your story matters.

2. Don't waste time comparing your story to others. *Comparison is the thief of joy* (Theodore Roosevelt). Avoid deflating your story because you think it's "average" – countless people will relate to your "average" story of struggle and challenges because they're experiencing similar situations.

3. Acknowledge that there are LEVELS of all knowledge and expertise and that there are people seeking access to the level of knowledge and expertise that you currently possess.

4. Abandon "Imposter Syndrome." Affirm for yourself daily that you are enough, you are worthy, and you are capable of being at the front of the room to share your voice as an expert, even with your flaws and imperfections. Trying to be perfect will always be an unachievable goal!

5. Celebrate your past instead of running from your past. Don't hide in shame or guilt about anything you've experienced in your life. Everything you've been through that didn't break you was meant to make you stronger. You have firsthand knowledge of overcoming obstacles and setbacks in life that will help someone else.

Remember, we each have our own unique set of experiences and perspectives, which means each of us has something of unique value to share. There will be people in the world who will only be magnetized to YOUR voice and who will not experience their transformation towards a better, more fulfilled life until they hear YOU.

To **own your story** means you acknowledge the transformational impact of everything you've been through, and you embrace that *your story is ABOUT you, but it ain't FOR you.* You take ownership of your authentic truth and use it to inspire others. **Giving power to your voice** means you are intentional about speaking up to "make your life bigger than you" by sharing what you know as a blueprint for those who are looking for a solution to their pain. It means instead of 'hoarding' the hurt you've experienced, you turn it into a master plan for someone else's healing. In effect, you become the prescription for somebody else's pain.

The following eight principles will support you on your journey to "cracking the success code" through public speaking:

PRINCIPLE #1: MASTERY
Take time to master your message and become a subject matter expert. People are inclined to listen, learn, and glean from individuals seen as authorities in their fields. They want to receive viable solutions from a Specialist, not a Generalist. Identify the topic, message, or subject matter you want to specialize in and become an avid student of that specialty. This will allow you to speak to others at your highest capacity.

PRINCIPLE #2: CLARITY
Get clear about your topic, message, or subject matter expertise and who you predominantly want to serve with your knowledge. Ask yourself:

- What do I *want* to teach?
- What am I *equipped* to teach?
- What topic, message, or subject matter have I mastered?

- Who is my target audience?
- What is the pain that my target audience is looking to relieve?
- What are the specific solutions I can offer to my target audience to resolve that pain?
- Where will I find my target audience?

PRINCIPLE #3: VISIBILITY

Visibility will always trump Ability. Even with a powerful story and message, if you aren't visible in today's marketplace, especially through social media, you will be a best-kept secret, and that will stifle your impact and your profitability. Identify the places where your target audience prefers to engage, and leverage those spaces to inform, educate, and inspire them. Stay at the top of their minds.

PRINCIPLE #4: AUTHENTICITY

Be yourself; everyone else is already taken (Oscar Wilde). As you begin sharing your story and your voice, show up as the genuine, authentic you. You are enough just as you are! Avoid trying to walk, talk, sound, or look like any other speaker. The best way to experience stellar results is by showing up as the authentic you, with your unique voice and delivery style.

PRINCIPLE #5: TRANSPARENCY

When sharing your story and providing guidance for individuals who are magnetized to your voice, share both your mess and your success. Be transparent and vulnerable in sharing your struggles, failures, and mistakes. Sharing your mess will resonate with audiences and allow people to see themselves in your story. Your mess is your *connection* with people, and your success is your *credibility* with people.

PRINCIPLE #6: CONSISTENCY

Consistency is all about repetition. In order to own your story and give power to your voice, you must consistently practice sharing your story in public, consistently share your voice on a variety of public platforms, and consistently work on the skill set of speaking publicly to create impact with your message.

PRINCIPLE #7: CREDIBILITY

Your credibility is equivalent to your reputation. A positive reputation in public speaking is developed by serving people well, educating and inspiring them. You want to develop the Know, Like, and Trust factor by overdelivering on the solutions that will help people achieve their desired results.

PRINCIPLE #8: PROFITABILITY

As you are sharing your knowledge and subject matter expertise, you never have to choose whether you will serve OR sell – you have permission to do BOTH. You deserve to be highly compensated for how well you serve. So, be sure to package your knowledge, then put a price tag on it... and add tax.

Your story and your voice are more powerful than you know! Now is the time to speak up, speak out, and maximize your knowledge to create global impact on the lives of others. Every experience you've encountered and lesson you've learned was intended to serve the world in a bigger way. I challenge you to own your story and give power to your voice, to help shape people's perspectives, educate and inform them, breathe life into their dreams, and shift the trajectory of their lives by teaching them what you know.

About Dr. Cheryl

Dr. Cheryl Wood is an International Empowerment Speaker, 2x TEDx Speaker, 17x Best-Selling Author, Leadership Expert, and Executive Speaker Development Coach. She specializes in equipping women with the tools to unleash the power of their voices, transform lives with their stories, and monetize their subject matter expertise. She empowers women to get out of their comfort zones, take calculated risks, pursue their big dreams, and become the best version of themselves as they powerfully use their voice to impact lives. Dr. Wood has trained countless women leaders across the United States and abroad in South Africa, India, France, United Kingdom, Jamaica, Canada, The Bahamas, Trinidad and Tobago, Bermuda, and Antigua, to name a few.

Dr. Wood is also the Founder of SpeakerCon, the premier annual conference, convention, and awards gala designed for communication experts to learn, grow, connect and celebrate the power of "transforming the world one word at a time." Participants include speakers, entrepreneurs, authors, coaches, consultants, media and radio personalities, educators, faith-based leaders, podcasters, poets, and advocates who are committed to unleashing the power of their voices to impact lives globally and to create an unforgettable legacy as they honor their God-given assignment and walk in their unique lanes of brilliance.

Dr. Wood has partnered with and shared the stage with some of the world's most influential thought leaders and industry experts, including Les Brown, Lisa Nichols, Trent Shelton, Dr. George Fraser, Gloria Mayfield Banks, Mikki Taylor, and Linda Clemons.

Dr. Wood has been featured on ABC, Radio One, *Forbes Magazine, Huffington Post, ESSENCE, Black Enterprise, Rolling Out, Sheen Magazine, Disruptor Magazine, Good Morning Washington,* Fox 5 News, Fox 45 News, *The Washington Informer, The Baltimore Times, Afro-American Newspaper,* and numerous other media outlets. She has delivered riveting keynote presentations for a host of organizations including NASA, Verizon, Capital One, The United Nations, United States Department of Defense, United States Department of Agriculture, National Association of Legal Professionals, Federally Employed Women, Blacks In Government, eWomen Network, the Congressional Black Caucus, and a host of law firms and national and international conferences. She has been featured on the cover of *SUCCESS Women's Magazine*, *SPEAKERS Magazine*, *Mogul Leaders Magazine*, and *Courageous Woman Magazine*. She was recognized as one of the Top 50 Most Influential Women by *VIP Global Magazine* and one of the Top 20 Entrepreneurs of 2021 by *Entrepreneurs Herald*.

Dr. Wood is committed to empowering and equipping women globally to make their unique fingerprint count and to create a living legacy starting today!

Learn more at:
- www.CherylEmpowers.com
- www.SpeakerconConference.com

Engage with her at:
- https://www.facebook.com/groups/gsugroup

Connect on all social media platforms at:
    @CherylEmpowers

CHAPTER 3

ARE TOXIC INFLUENCERS POISONING YOU AND YOUR DREAMS?

BY IRENE NAKAMURA

In 2010, when I was diagnosed with cancer, I'd spent decades in toxic relationships - with my family, my friends, and my profession.

My life was literally killing me.

Faced with my own mortality, change was the only cure. I needed to stop allowing toxic people, experiences, and environments to dictate who I was, the work I did, and how I spent my time. I had to reclaim the years of my life lost to toxic influencers who controlled my life, chose my future, and determined my worth. My self-sabotaging mindset had set me up for failure after failure. It wasn't until my life was on the line and I was undergoing post-cancer-surgery radiation that I saw what was at stake. It was time to make a change. I needed to take inventory of my values and figure out why I not only gave toxic influencers space in my life, but why I'd let them control me for so long.

TRAPPED BY TRADITION

Although I was raised in America, Japanese culture was prevalent in my life. As proud as I am of the culture, some of its cultural and societal norms set strict rules and conventions on both my behavior and my choices. My future was chosen for me. My husband was chosen for me. My role and destiny were chosen for me. I was expected to put my career, dreams, and future on hold and support my brother. As the male in the family, his education, career, and future were not only more important than mine, but they were also a prerequisite for mine. This subservient role had been hard-wired into my brain from a young age by my mother. She had, after all, done the same for her brother in Japan. In the male-dominated Japanese society, there was only one place for women - behind men.

I vividly recall a time in high school, wondering why I should put in the effort to remain at the top of my class. My brother, five years younger than me, would have all the benefits of my hard work. I should just give up. According to my mother's mandate and that of my culture, I could only begin to pursue my education after my brother completed his. It was my responsibility to support him in every way possible. In fact, by the time he received his double Master's Ivy League education, at the age of 31, I had paid for the majority of it. Not just with my hard-earned dollars but with my future.

There is a word in Japanese, *gaman* (pronounced gah-mahn), which means to tolerate or put up with. The idea of 'sucking it up' was part of my DNA. I had mastered that skill, but it hadn't broken my spirit.

PATHS ARE CHOSEN, NOT DETERMINED

Despite the path my family mapped out for me, I wanted another path. Against my mother's wishes, I enrolled in a trade school and began training as a court reporter. For ten years, I worked my way through the ranks. My starting salary of just $40,000 working part-time grew to an impressive $450,000, and the opportunities to earn more seemed endless.

Of course, most of this income was not mine to enjoy. As my family and culture mandated, there were my brother's college expenses and those of my family to cover. In nearly the same time it took my brother to receive his prestigious education, I was earning six figures. I was in high demand, and I was the first Japanese American official court reporter for the United States District Court, Central District of California, a position I'd worked tirelessly to earn.

But despite my success, I still allowed toxic influencers to derail me. Just five years into this role, the judge, who was my long-time mentor and advocate, and whose principles and respect I regarded above all others, reached senior status. The combination of his age and years on the bench totaled 80. With a significantly reduced caseload, he was no longer allowed a dedicated court reporter. I was reassigned. The new judge, while a competent and fervent protector of the law, did not match up, for me, to the level of his predecessor. This new position didn't suit me. The environment at the courthouse had become increasingly toxic as well. The already competitive workplace was mired in backstabbing, sabotage, and personal vendettas. I chose to put myself first and step down.

While the choice should have been mine, it wasn't. Acting as the dedicated court reporter for a US District Judge garnered prestige. Although my career and prestigious position were attained against their wishes and the dictates of my culture, I'd finally earned their respect. Leaving a position of such prestige was considered an insult. Ironically, the same people who hadn't respected my decision to carve my own path now felt they had a right to dictate its direction. Some members of my family shunned me. Some still don't speak to me nearly 15 years later.

I accepted a position at a new company, but my efforts to break free from a toxic workplace were short-lived. The new firm had strict expedited deadlines for transcripts, and they offered these services for free at the court reporter's expense.

The winter holiday was approaching, and I'd just received some frightening news – a cancer diagnosis. My shock was compounded when the company's scheduling coordinator approached me with a special client request to take on a multi-party case with a demanding lawyer with whom I'd previously developed a rapport. It was a client they wanted to please at any cost. I agreed on the condition that the job would not interfere with my scheduled surgery or recovery. I was assured it wouldn't and agreed to take the job. Though my mind should have been focused on my health and impending surgery, I remained professional and did my due diligence, connecting with each of the approximately 40 lawyers working on the case. Each agreed to allow the final transcripts to be turned in after the holiday. With everything in order, I left for the hospital with the hopes I'd be leaving the toxic cancer behind and starting fresh.

The surgery was successful. My doctors removed the toxic invader from my body. I was elated. I returned from the hospital, however, to find numerous emails and a full voicemail box. The messages complained of my unprofessionalism, ungratefulness, and thoughtlessness for not returning calls. These issues were not ones I was able to address from my hospital, nor were they part of our originally agreed-upon arrangement. Although I was now cancer-free, toxicity continued to invade my life.

REDIRECT YOUR MINDSET TO CLARIFY YOUR PATH

As I began radiation treatments, the cumulative effect of toxicity in my life overwhelmed me. I wanted my own identity, to earn my own income, to be successful, and be independent.

Sometimes bad things happen to allow you to clarify your path.

They help you see the challenges in front of you, to face them, and become the person you want to be. Perhaps my cancer diagnosis was just that. I no longer wanted to be a victim of the choices others made for me. I vowed to start my own company and create an environment where people were treated with empathy, compassion, and equity. I wanted it to be a workplace that empowered people and gave them the freedom to make their own decisions, a place where they were treated fairly and where race, religion, gender, and life choices had no bearing on their ability to do a good job.

From this place of newfound clarity, iDepo was born. In its first year, iDepo had two clients and made less than $10K, but I felt empowered. Ten years later, the company is nationally certified, as well as specially certified in five states, and as a minority- and woman-owned business. My offices in California, Washington State, and Hawaii have 15 full-time employees and hundreds of contracted court reporters. Last year, iDepo recorded seven figures in gross sales.

My journey has taught me valuable lessons. Surrounding yourself with toxic influencers makes it easy for their negative thinking to derail you. Often, it takes a galvanizing event to clearly see the level of toxicity and its effects on your life. Unfortunately for me, that clarity was a cancer diagnosis. It was only after releasing and replacing toxic relationships and environments that my life changed, and my business grew exponentially.

IDENTIFY YOUR TOXIC INFLUENCERS

The first step in ridding yourself of toxic influencers is to identify them. This requires an understanding of how they behave, recognizing how they sound and what actions they take. But even with this information, you must be willing to take action to protect yourself.

Can you identify these five types of toxic influencers in YOUR life?

1. The Naysayer

Takes away your freedom to attain, implement, or come up with new and fresh ideas. Keeps you in your comfort zone by preying on your fears, anxieties, judgments, and sensitivities.

— "What will they say about you?"
— "What will they say about me that I allowed/supported you to do this?"
— "You're only setting yourself up for failure. Why even try."

2. The Energy Vampire

Sucks the energy from you and your ideas. May appear to be supportive but often find ways to pour negativity onto your dreams.

— "How are you going to make any money doing that?"
— "Sounds like a lot of work."
— "Great idea! It's a pity you can't do/handle it."

3. The Dream Slayer

Outright tells you not to pursue an idea. That it's stupid, a waste of time, or not attainable.

— "You don't have the experience/credentials to do that."
— "What a dumb idea."

4. The Idea Thief

Highly competitive and attempts to talk you out of your dreams so they can take your ideas. Often masquerades as a friend or confidant, allowing them to fly under your radar. Harmful to you for their own gain.

— "Don't go for that job. I heard bad things about that company."

— "Sounds like a good idea, but don't you think I could do a better job than you?"

5. The Control Capturer

Feels entitled and frequently uses tactics such as belittling or aggressive or foul language. Makes unreasonable demands that cannot be met. Nothing you do is good enough. May show up as a high-maintenance client.

— "We shouldn't have to pay for that extra service. It should just be included."

— "If you don't bend the rules the way I want, I'll prevent others from using your services."

Once you've identified the type of toxic influencer in your life, ask yourself these questions.

o Are you allowing them to dictate your narrative by impacting your decisions or making decisions for you?

o Do you need the validation of your influencer so much that you're willing to forgo your own needs, wants, and dreams to please or appease them?

o Are you giving away your power?

Remember, toxic influencers need your permission to take control.

ELIMINATE TOXIC INFLUENCERS BY TAKING BACK YOUR POWER

1) Set boundaries.

Distance yourself and don't allow them to limit your goals, dreams, and joy.

2) Don't normalize their toxic behaviors.

Remove them from your conversations or your life. Limit your time with these people.

3) Stop self-sabotaging by asking for their opinions.

4) Actively and completely remove toxic influencers from your life.

Cut the cancer out and take their power away.

- ○ If your toxic influencer is a family member or someone who must remain in your life, minimize communication with them regarding your dreams and goals. Find alternative ways to communicate. Better yet, leave the conversation or redirect it toward neutral topics. Redirect the power.
- ○ If your toxic influencer is a business associate, ask yourself, "Is the business partner, employee, or client worth it?" Set boundaries for your business interactions. Create an exit strategy that allows you to be in control.

5) Step into your discomfort zone, so you can step into your target zone.

6) Replace a toxic influencer with a positive uplifter who empowers you and your ideas.

RECAPTURE YOUR POWER

Once you've eliminated the toxic influencer or their effects from your life, you can begin to refocus your efforts. Examine your goals to identify what's preventing you from achieving them.

- ○ Find a true supporter and spend more time with them and other positive, like-minded people.
- ○ Read books by authors successful in life, health, and business, or watch inspirational content.
- ○ Begin a program to improve your mindset by handwriting affirmations and gratitudes every day.
- ○ Join empowerment and mindset enhancement groups.
- ○ Hire a mentor/business coach to help you navigate away from toxic influencers and toward self-powering generators.

Free yourself to pursue YOUR dreams. Even if you struggle with feelings of inadequacy, do it anyway.

Watch how your business and life transform! You will feel empowered to pursue that big client, open that second store or company, launch that new product idea, or even pivot your business altogether.

Reclaim your power and crack the success code that aligns with you and your dreams. Break free from toxic influencers and focus on you and your business on your terms.

What does a toxic influencer-free life look like to you?

About Irene

Irene Nakamura is the founder and CEO of iDepo Reporters, a full-service, nationally certified court reporting and litigation support company with offices in three states. Irene has built a nationwide team of more than 1,000 court reporters by offering a personal and professional work environment that values the individual first. iDepo Reporters is empowered to personalize and customize services for each client. "We treat each case, no matter the size, as if it were our only one."

Unwilling to be complacent with the status quo, Irene defied the suppressive conventions of her traditional Japanese upbringing and its relegation of women to the background to pursue her dreams. While providing financial support for her parents and brother and funding her brother's Ivy League education, Irene bootstrapped her way through court reporting school. In the ten years that followed, she garnered a reputation that put her in high demand and allowed her to generate a six-figure income. She overcame racial biases by becoming the first Japanese American Official Court Reporter for the United States District Court for the Central District of California.

When a cancer diagnosis threatened her life, Irene faced it with the same tenacity she had the societal and cultural pressures leveled against her. She stared it down and won. Her diagnosis propelled her to make drastic changes in her life – leave a toxic work environment, end her selected marriage, and start and run her own 7-figure business.

The journey brought about a new clarity, one she channels not only into her personal life but also her professional life. "I am not merely a survivor; I'm a thriver." Her battle with cancer gave her the power to step out of her comfort zone and tell her story, something she would have never done due to fear of judgment and anxiety. "Now I live my life for me, not merely doing things in order to please others."

An out-of-the-box thinker, Irene is always looking for opportunities to empower others, especially women and minorities. She's particularly proud of her culturally diverse iDepo team.

Irene's non-profit work includes pro bono clinics for CASA Career Day, for children aging out of the foster care system, and Gardena Pioneer Project, a non-profit that provides services to Japanese Seniors. iDepo has supported the Hawaiian Paralegals Association, Women Lawyers Association of Los Angeles, National Asian Pacific American Bar Association, Japanese American Bar Association, and National Association of Minority and Women Owned Law Firms and many more.

Irene is an active member of the National Court Reporters Association and the Deposition Reporters Association.

iDepo provides litigation services, including document retrieval, process service, subpoenas, stenographic court reporting, transcriptions, trial presentation, and legal videography, as well as translation and interpreter services. Like Irene, her company is resilient, responding to the ever-changing business landscape by offering remote training for legal professionals and providing moderators who deal with the logistics of remote depositions, exhibit presentation, and technical issues.

Contact Irene at:
- www.IreneNakamura.com
- LinkedIn: https://www.linkedin.com/in/irene-nakamura/
- Website: https://ideporeporters.com/
- Instagram: @irene_nakamura_tabascogirley
- Facebook: facebook.com/irenenakamura
- Clubhouse @inyidepo

CHAPTER 4

MINDSET HACKS: DEVELOPING AN ENTREPRENEURIAL MINDSET

BY RACHEL WITHERS

Success means something different to everyone. Each of us has a vision for our future that we would like to make a reality. To design the business that we want, we must first define the life goals into which that business must fit. Most people conceive of a business plan by thinking of something they think will make money, and they might think it counterintuitive to worry about how their business will fit into their current life and personal goals. Entrepreneurs are often reminded to "keep their eyes on the prize" to sharpen their focus on building their business, but what is the prize? The prize, how a person measures success, is the foundation of the entrepreneurial mindset.

We are each born with a special purpose and the talents and passion to bring that purpose to fruition. If we don't do everything in our power to see those passions translate into our reality, then we rob ourselves and the rest of the world of the beauty that only we can create. Richard Branson recently

CRACKING THE SUCCESS CODE - VOL 2

flew to space, realizing one of his childhood dreams. Had Branson told himself that the dream of reaching space was too lofty a goal, he would likely have given up, depriving himself and others of achieving that goal. Instead, his entrepreneurial mindset absolutely thought the sky is the limit. There is no reason why you can't achieve your most outrageous goals, too. Entrepreneurs like Branson are no different from you, except they've learned how to nurture their mindset. They have learned to think like an entrepreneur, and so can anyone with a vision and the passion to succeed.

You might assume that I have always been in business, always identified with an entrepreneurial mindset. I assure you; I have not. Ballet was my first career and my earliest passion. Ballet made my mind and body happy, which naturally allowed me to bring a positive mindset to my day-to-day life. After I had two kids, I left ballet behind, got a divorce, faced life challenges, and slowly lost my sense of self. My mind and body were neglected and no longer happy. To reconnect with the joy of ballet, I began to incorporate old ballet moves into my daily routine. Before I knew it, I had built a fitness routine around my passion for ballet. As I slowly fell in love with ballet again, it dawned on me that other women could benefit from my fitness method too. BalletBeFit was born. Initially, I stuck with what I knew. I offered classes and developed a training program for instructors.

As my business grew, so did my entrepreneurial mindset. Just a few years ago, I would not have imagined being where I am today. I operate my ballet-inspired fitness brand, BalletBeFit, run a seven-figure property company, am the founder of a business growth hub, and help other business owners, entrepreneurs, and service providers who are struggling to align their marketing strategies with their business objectives. Something miraculous happened that first day I returned to ballet – I found my passion again and lit a fire for my future growth.

To me, being an entrepreneur means finding that drive within yourself to bring something powerful to life. It's about being inspired by what you do. Developing an entrepreneurial mindset is a practice, like yoga or ballet. The more you flex your mindset muscles, the nimbler and more natural your responses become. Any practice is based on exercises. Ten exercises have supercharged my business and those of my coaching clients. You have nothing to lose by putting these hacks into practice to change your mindset and supercharge your business.

1. Believe in Yourself

To become a successful entrepreneur, you need to believe in yourself and your ideas. This may sound obvious, but it is crucial to get it right because your beliefs hold significant power. When you are confident in your vision, you operate in a way that will bring it to life, and you are prepared to take risks because you believe in your ideas. Think of a famous entrepreneur that you admire. Whether it's Elon Musk or Oprah Winfrey, Duncan Bannatyne, or Arianna Huffington, these people all have something in common. They are incredibly confident and believe wholeheartedly in their product or business. If you cultivate an unwavering sense of self-belief, you will be able to survive the ups and downs of being an entrepreneur. Self-belief buoys you through the challenging days. On good days, you will know it's because you believed in yourself enough to get there. Celebrate the small victories. The more you acknowledge how far you have come, the more self-belief you will be able to cultivate. The small wins are just as important as the big ideas behind them. Believing in yourself means you are not afraid to go after your dreams, no matter how big and outlandish they may seem, so think big.

2. Think Big

Yes! Great entrepreneurs are not afraid to think big! Big does not necessarily mean money. What success means to one person may mean something completely different to someone else. You might not be concerned about owning a flashy car but desire a comfortable lifestyle that enables you to look after your family and to have the time to enjoy a nice holiday. Big might mean the ability to structure your own workday and the ability to choose the people with whom you work. Thinking big means pushing your fears to the side and daring to pursue that dream business without allowing any excuse to hold you back.

Too often, we are trained to worry about consequences, which, of course, has its place. Entrepreneurs run with ideas while the rest of the world ponders the potential downfalls. *They haven't even got it all figured out; they just go with it and learn along the way.* Thinking big is about going all-in on your ideas, giving them one hundred percent of your attention and faith. Why wouldn't you operate this way? If you give an idea your all, and it doesn't work out, at least you can say with certainty that you did your very best. You can feel proud and walk away with your head held high, ready to put everything you learned into your next venture. If you succeed? Well, then you get to embrace that sweet sense of victory completely! It will feel even better knowing you pursued your most daring dream and breathed it into existence.

3. Focus

Big ideas require focus. When you're pursuing an exciting new business venture, achieving a high level of focus is crucial for your success. The first part of this is eliminating distractions, procrastination, and excuses. There will always be one billion reasons why you shouldn't start. Behind that procrastination is fear. You're delaying action because the outcome feels scary or daunting. Learn to notice this quickly and pivot back to the main goal.

To do this effectively, you need to zero in on your goals. If you need to write a business plan, what are the steps you need to take? If you're trying to scale your business, what are the first steps? Make a list of everything you need to do to be successful in the current phase of your business. You can make this list as long as you want. Commit your thoughts to paper and then pare it down from there. Circle the top five most important things that you can do now and get started. Turning a giant goal into a few smaller, actionable steps will help you stay focused.

4. Make Quick Decisions

Emotions can become tangled up in our decisions. Successful entrepreneurs avoid emotion-driven decision-making. Emotions are certainly a part of life, but when it comes to decisions, they can slow the process and hinder progress. Entrepreneurs must act quickly, even if they do not feel ready. They trade a bit of discomfort in the hope that they produce something their target audience finds new, fresh, and daring. Cutting-edge products like Apple computers would never come about if entrepreneurs like Steve Jobs spent years weighing their options.

Former U.S. Secretary of State and retired General Colin Powell used a 40-70 rule of swift decision making. He said a person needs no less than 40 percent and no more than 70 percent of the information available before deciding. With less than 40 percent of the information needed, you will probably make the wrong choice. However, if a person waits until they acquire 70 percent of the data, they could miss their window of opportunity. No businessperson wants the competition to get to market first with their idea. Swift decision-making isn't just good for business, it's also essential for leadership. A team needs to know that their leader trusts himself enough to decide without delay. Making quick decisions is easy when you trust yourself.

5. Trust Your Gut

Albert Einstein, one of the most brilliant scientific minds, said, "The only real valuable thing is intuition." Learning to trust that inner wisdom is crucial to finding business success. Learn to be comfortable not having all the facts in front of you. Follow your gut instinct and let that guide you on your path.

If you're like me, you're passionate about your business idea. Instinct told me that many other women would benefit from my new fitness method. I believed that fellow ballet lovers would jump at the opportunity to teach these classes, too. Usually, the idea you developed came from your desire to put something good into the world. Your intuition got you where you are now, so have the confidence to bring it with you into your decision-making processes. Trusting your gut ultimately saves you time, and time is valuable.

6. Protect Your Time

The next step in developing an entrepreneurial mindset is to learn to value and protect your time. As they say, time is money, and that's a big reason why I encouraged entrepreneurs to conquer procrastination and eliminate distractions. What better way to guard your time and ensure every second generates as much value as possible?

Is that long lunch meeting going to be productive or distracting? Is checking your emails for the tenth time helpful, or is it depleting your time bank? Make a point to ask yourself these questions and adjust your daily routines accordingly. This doesn't mean work nonstop. Know your limits and schedule breaks accordingly. Rest is a valuable use of your time if it is scheduled and not a means of distraction. A good entrepreneur knows precisely how they are spending their hours and uses time wisely to generate as much value as possible for their business and those that it serves.

7. Ask How You Can Provide Value to Others

This practice will surely change how you approach business. Instead of asking how your business can serve you, ask how you can provide value for others. President John F. Kennedy famously said: "Ask not what your country can do for you, ask what you can do for your country."

These aren't just good words for a political leader to live by, they are crucial for entrepreneurs as well. Great businesses are not self-centered. They focus on how to solve a customer's problem and make the target consumer the center of their focus. Creating value boosts loyalty and trust, generates leads, stimulates growth, and makes you feel great about your business. You can practice this in all kinds of decisions throughout your day. Is your social media output focused on you or your audience? Are you doing a lot of talking about showing up for your clients, or are you showing up for them with useful information and prompt solutions? If you're planning for your business, ask yourself if the decision will provide more value to others. Great entrepreneurs never stop asking this question and always yearn to increase the value they offer their clients, team members, and business partners.

8. Conduct Regular Mental Check-Ins

Ensure while you are providing value to others in your business that you don't forget to periodically check in with yourself. It's easy to think that you have entirely nailed the entrepreneurial mindset, but some behaviors or thoughts are sure to trip you up now and again. Check your mindset regularly. Sit down and ask yourself if you are focused. What is motivating you? Do you feel as confident as you could in your day-to-day decisions?

You can do these check-ins however you prefer. Meeting up with a mentor, jotting down some notes, or holding a meeting with team members to discuss mindset are all effective check-ins. Being an entrepreneur means wearing one hundred hats a day and working long hard hours. It is easy to fall into survival mode. Maintaining some form of personal evaluation keeps your values and priorities in focus no matter how many challenges you face or how many times you fail.

9. See Failure as An Opportunity for Growth

An entrepreneur does not dwell on failure. When failures happen, they see them as opportunities to learn and grow. Entrepreneurs rarely achieve success without a few setbacks along the way, and if they let that stop them, they would never see success.

Learning to accept failure involves not letting your ego get the better of you. Entrepreneurship is quite a vulnerable role, and it's easy to want to put your guard up or hide failures from the world. Failure makes you better. Failure means you're evolving your vision and learning what works and what doesn't. You get to take all of that new knowledge and apply it to your next endeavor. You don't get these insights from playing it safe. Value the knowledge born from adversity. You're in the best company. After all, it is the rare entrepreneur who has not messed up, gone bust, or had an issue somewhere along the way.

10. Keep Your Eye on the Prize

Successful entrepreneurs keep their eye on the prize. Even moving one inch a day is better than standing still. If you keep your vision in sight, you can stay motivated enough to persevere through anything. Steve Jobs once said, *"I'm convinced that about half of what separates the successful entrepreneurs from the non-successful ones is pure perseverance... Unless you have a lot of passion about this, you're not going to survive. You're going to give it up. So, you've got to have an idea, or a problem or a wrong that you want to right that you're passionate about;*

otherwise, you're not going to have the perseverance to stick it through." Every time things get tough, redirect your eye toward the core reasons you started this endeavor in the first place.

Whether you are an entrepreneur in a slump or a person with a big idea and the passion to power it, you can develop the mindset to become a successful entrepreneur filled with pride and purpose. Become stronger than the fears that limit you and achieve bigger success than you have imagined.

About Rachel

Rachel Withers helps people around the world make mindset, lifestyle, and business changes needed to achieve their dreams.

As a business strategist, serial entrepreneur, and public speaker, Rachel applies her experience to coach clients towards personal empowerment and thriving careers. She is the founder of the successful fitness concept BalletBeFit, director of a successful property company, and founder and CEO of business training academy 'Business Growth Hub.'

After founding the successful fitness concept BalletBeFit, Rachel has used her experience to encourage others. Through her courses, Rachel teaches personal development, mindset, wealth mastery, and business development to help each client gain control of their health, wellbeing, career, and finances.

As a public speaker, she captivates audiences around the world with tried and tested strategies for empowerment and growth. Rachel supports people as they build a sense of confidence and learn to apply it within their private and public lives.

Rachel is an Amazon #1 bestselling author, with her book *Become a FITPreneur*, and has co-authored with the world's leading entrepreneurs and professionals, including Jack Canfield, to reveal their success secrets with the best seller book, *Success*.

Rachel is a former dancer, who trained with the Royal Ballet, and holds a Bachelor of Performance Arts from Leeds University. She has studied and worked with numerous notable dancers.

When Rachel's dance career ended and she became a mum, her self-esteem took a hit. She realised she needed to make a change for both herself and her family. By transforming her mindset, she used her dance background to develop her ballet-based fitness method BalletBeFit. This mental shift allowed her to surpass career and fitness goals, inspire women to build businesses, and teach her strategies to students worldwide.

On her path to success, Rachel has worked with incredible mentors such as Pat Mesiti and Bob Proctor. She continues harnessing the insights she learned along the way by creating dynamic content for her followers. She hosts the monthly series *Mindset Matters* on the Success Channel, which has top speakers such as Brian Tracy, Jack Canfield, and Nick Nanton, and uses her experiences and personal development as a way to connect with audiences at her inspirational public speaking engagements. Rachel has been featured on ABC, NBC, CBS, and Fox affiliates around the country as a guest of Hollywood live.

Rachel believes we all have what it takes to live the life we deserve. She uses the lessons of her journey to deliver quick results, help her clients discover how to pursue their passion, gain their personal power, and surpass their visions of success and how to implement proven marketing and business strategies. Through Rachel's resources, people learn how to accelerate their progress and self-worth through the power of transforming their mindset combined with entrepreneurship.

Connect with Rachel at:
- info@rachelwithershq.co.uk
- www.rachelwithershq.co.uk
- www.twitter.com/rachelwithershq
- www.facebook.com/rachelwithershq
- www.instagram.com/rachelwithershq
- www.youtube.com/c/RachelWithersHQ

CHAPTER 5

SUCCESSFULLY SELL YOUR IDEAS™
CRACKING THE CODE OF LEGALLY OWNING YOUR IDEAS AND DEMYSTIFYING THE PROCESS OF VALUATION AND COMMERCIALIZATION

BY KATHRYN WILLIAMS

Today the most valuable assets are more likely to be stored in the cloud than in a warehouse.[1]
~ Dame Inga Beale

Whether you are an architect, inventor, owner of a trade secret, designer, author, or your name is on the shingle above your store – your ideas can become global success stories worth millions of dollars.

---

1. Today the most valuable assets are more likely to be stored in the cloud than in a warehouse." Inga Beale, Chief Executive Officer of Lloyd's of London. "Intangible assets are twice as valuable as tangible assets across 19 different industries and represents a substantial portion of many companies' overall value." World Intellectual Property Organization Study and Report.

Ideas are intangible – known as intellectual property – they are a 'product' of your intellect and considered 'property', like land, just not tangible.

As a society, we have progressed from farmers and manufacturers into the digital information and knowledge economy, seeing the rise of startups like Facebook, Airbnb, and Canva, whose value lies not in physical assets but rather their intangible assets.

Like the founders of these successful businesses, millions of people come up with clever ideas every day. Yet, most are unaware of the simple yet powerful steps they should take to legally own and protect their intellectual property. This conundrum has fuelled my curiosity and subsequent research over the past 20 years, giving rise to this chapter about *The Idea Lifecycle*™ – a simple four-step process to crack the code to successfully identify, protect, and sell your ideas.

Read on to become well informed of your legal rights and commercial opportunities.

THE IDEA LIFECYCLE™

What has value?

Most businesses have a range of asset types, which are split into two categories: tangible assets and intangible assets.

Tangible assets include cash, inventory, raw materials, equipment, and real estate, and most of us understand how they are valued. Take Nike, for example, these assets would include their bank accounts, physical offices, factories, and inventory.

Unlike physical products, you cannot actually touch an intangible asset – like technology, brand, design, or creative concepts. However, that doesn't mean they don't have value. Just consider what it might cost to acquire Nike's swoosh logo or what Nike pays their lawyers to protect it.

While many ideas have the potential to become valuable intangible assets, there is a clear four-step process:

The Idea Lifecycle™ tracks ideas from inception to implementation:

1. **Ideation**
2. **Protection**
3. **Valuation**
4. **Sale**

So, take a piece of paper and a pen, and let's work through the transition of your idea from something that only exists in your mind to an asset that can be sold for a profit.

STEP 1. THE IDEA

The first stage of *The Idea Lifecycle™* is the core idea itself. Although the idea may not yet be fully formed, even at this early stage, your idea is potentially valuable.

Idea theft is a real concern, particularly for innovators and creative agencies who pitch their ideas to prospects and clients because once seen, it is impossible to 'un-see' an idea, which could be replicated and stolen.

- *The value of IP:*

  It might surprise you that an idea can have value in two distinct ways – through its registration as unique protected intellectual property, as well as through its execution.

  One way to think about this distinction is to compare your intellectual property to the title deed for a block of land. You may have an idea for a beautiful mansion, but without purchasing the title deed to the land, you cannot execute that idea by building the mansion on the land. The title deed is a necessary cost to bring your idea to life, but it is separate from the cost of the mansion, and it can be sold with or without the mansion on it.

Similarly, when you have an idea, the cost of protecting the intellectual property is separate from time and material costs involved in executing the idea. However, like a title deed, once your idea is registered as intellectual property, it can be valued and sold, whether it is executed or not.

▪ *The value of execution:*

The execution of your idea is when it finds its real-world implementation. It is when Nike's swoosh is affixed to its apparel and equipment, Airbnb's founders built the website through which users could book beds, or when Tiffany & Co. apply their trademarked blue to gift boxes and carry bags. From a business perspective, once an intellectual property attribute has been implemented in this way, the intellectual property directly contributes to business results, meaning – the value of the intellectual property itself increases as the value of the business does.

This brings us to the ultimate intangible asset – a business's brand. A brand is the result of a suite of intangible assets designed to enhance the connection between producer and consumer by adding 'value' to commercial utility through aesthetic design, attractive packaging, a feeling combined with alluring images, memorable jingles, and catchy slogans, with one single goal in mind: to get you to buy their product or service.

A strong brand resonates with consumers, delivering customer loyalty, increased sales, premium pricing, and dedicated employees. This is why world-famous brands continue to invest in intangible assets, registering their intellectual property rights and fiercely protecting them from competitors.

Get started today, list down your intangible assets, then move on to Step 2: Develop a strategy to protect them.

STEP 2. PROTECTION

Some ideas have inherent value, which is why venture capitalists invest, and entrepreneurs like you are inspired to create new businesses, technologies, and art. However, without legal ownership and protection, your ideas can be stolen.

Dragons' Den

Do not share ideas with anyone until you have protected the intellectual property attributes of your idea. Many learn this the hard way, as seen in the Dragons' Den television show, where budding entrepreneurs present their ideas to the 'Dragons' (the venture capitalists) trying to convince any one of the Dragons to invest money into their business idea. Some of the first questions the Dragons ask are:

- Do you own the idea?
- Have you registered your rights?

If the Dragons discover the entrepreneur's idea has not been legally protected, they call: "I'm out" and are not willing to invest.

The intention of legally protecting intellectual property serves both you as the owner by awarding you exclusive legal rights, adding to brand equity and business valuation; and also, the consumer who relies on the source and quality of the brand promise made to them. However, the intangible nature of intellectual property presents difficulties when compared with traditional property like land and goods.

If you are a landowner, you can mark out the perimeter and surround your land with a fence, CCTV and hire armed guards to protect it. If you own a shop, you can attach security tags to your products and hire security staff to stand at the front door. On the other hand, as a creator of intellectual property, you cannot apply the same measures to protect your intangible assets. Once seen, an idea cannot be un-seen. Unless you have adequate protections in place, you can do little to stop others from copying your idea.

Ideas cannot be expressed without first occurring in the mind of the creator. However, once the idea leaves your mind and is transformed and fixed into a tangible medium, such as an audio recording, a written manuscript, or a doodle on a napkin, you can identify which aspects are considered valuable intellectual property and protected under the following legal regimes:

a) Copyright: original literary and artistic works.
b) Trademark: brand names and logos.
c) Design marks: appearance of a manufactured article.
d) Patent: new and useful inventions.
e) Trade secrets: valuable proprietary information.

Companies around the globe protect their intellectual property so they can commercialize these intangible assets. By 2019, there were: 15.2 million trademarks, 3.2 million patents, and 1.4 million industrial design applications.[2]

Many companies strategically register a suite of intellectual property rights in multiple regimes, for example:

Coca-Cola

1. Copyright: advertising and promotion strategies
2. Trademark: wordmarks for COCA-COLA and COKE
3. Patent: the shape of the bottle
4. Trade Secret: formula

The extent, duration, and cost of legal protection differs depending on the type of intellectual property. Without legal ownership, you

---

2. WIPO IP Facts and Figures 2020 - https://www.wipo.int/edocs/pubdocs/en
   wipo_pub_943_2020.pdf

run the risk of your intellectual property being stolen and having no legal recourse to do anything about it.

Now is the time to check: have you registered your intellectual property rights?

STEP 3. VALUATION

So important is intellectual property that owners are granted special protection rights to encourage creativity, innovation, and competition to benefit society and drive a strong economy.

Intangible assets are treated in the same way as tangible property: you can keep it, bequeath it, and commercialize it. However, even if you never intend to sell your intangible assets, that doesn't prevent them from being stolen or infringed upon. If you haven't valued your assets, how will you know the level of insurance you will need? How will you know if a particular asset is worth fighting for after you discover a theft or infringement? Probably not at all if you do not have legal ownership.

The rise in importance of intellectual property has seen an increase of consulting firms focusing on valuation and greater disclosure of financial details pertaining to intangible assets and their implied value.

Whilst there are more than 39 different proprietary valuation models[3] to assess fair value of intangible assets, there are three basic approaches:

  (i). **Cost**
  (ii). **Market**
  (iii). **Income**

---

3. The International Brand Valuation Manual, A complete overview and analysis of brand valuation techniques, methodologies, and applications. Gabriela Salinas 2009 John Wiley & Sons Ltd

(i). **Cost** approach

The cost approach is based on the question: What would you need to pay to replace or reproduce the asset today?

Costs might include:

• Concept development
• Intellectual property search and registration
• Design services
• Market research
• Advertising
• Promotion
• Licensing

Add up the costs involved in creating, protecting, and maintaining the asset, convert the amount into today's dollars, and presto – you have valued your intangible asset!

(ii). **Market** approach

The market approach measures value in comparison to transactions for a similar intangible asset. This method is like researching prices for similar houses in your suburb before putting a price on your own home. However, you will only know 'how much?' when the house is sold. The sale price is considered to be the market value - what a buyer will pay.

(iii). Future **Income**

Conceptually, the income approach is superior to the cost and market valuation models, as it addresses future business performance of the asset.

WhatsApp

As an example, startup business WhatsApp, which

was built entirely on intangible assets, was acquired by Facebook in 2014 for the landmark price of USD 21.8 billion, despite WhatsApp not yet delivering a profit.[4] It was not WhatsApp's bank balance that Facebook was buying, but rather the purchase price was based on future income projections anticipated from their 450 million users, which were growing by a million users every day.[5]

Grab your pen and paper – use the above methods to calculate the value of your intangible assets.

STEP 4. SALE

With legal rights to control intellectual property and an estimated fair value, you are now ready to commercialize.

Sales approach 1: Direct sale

Your first option for selling is simply making a one-off sale for the asset. This could be selling your logo design or strategic document for a fee charged for the idea itself even before the concept is produced and implemented.

If you are in the creative industry: ideation and strategic documents are your tools of trade. Therefore, it is imperative to know how much to price your ideas, separate and distinct from selling your time and materials to execute them. Here is an inspiring example:

Citibank

As part of the $10 million global execution campaign, Citibank paid $1.5 million for the logo.[6] You may think

4. https://www.investopedia.com/articles/investing/032515/whatsapp-best-face book-purchase-ever
5. Facebook buys WhatsApp for $19 billion by Adrian Covert @CNNTech February 19, 2014: 6:54 PM ET https://money.cnn.com/2014/02/19/ technology/ social/facebook-whatsapp/index.html
6. Five expensive logos and what they teach us, Tom May March 06, 2019. Creative Bloq https://www.creativebloq.com/features/5-expensive-logos and-what-they -teach-us

that this price is incredibly high; however, twenty years later, Citi was worth $32.2 million dollars and ranked 6th in the Top 10 Global Banking Brands.[7] Using the future revenue streams method, the Citibank logo remains the visual identification of the bank across all touchpoints used around the globe, and is likely to continue as the iconic brand image for many years to come, thus continuing to deliver returns on the original investment.

Sales approach 2: Licensing

Rather than an outright sale, a licence is a legal agreement to use someone else's intellectual property, whereby the owner retains the rights to their works and grants permission to use the work to promote the licensee's products or services for smaller instalments usually based on the number of sales.

Licensing provides enormous strategic, marketing, and earning benefits to both licensor and licensee. Both parties negotiate what they consider to be fair remuneration in exchange for the rights to exploit the intellectual property.

Licensing fees can be paid in a variety of ways:

(i). Lump-sum payment on signing the licence.
(ii). Milestone payments during the term of the licence.
(iii). Royalties calculated as a percentage of sales or profits.

According to Licensing International: licensing is the fastest and most profitable way to grow a business and maximize brand value in any industry, from major corporations to the smallest of small businesses. In fact, global sales of licensed products and services grew to USD 280.3 billion in 2019. Entertainment and characters is the largest category, with

7. Brand Finance Banking 500 2021 - Sber Named World's Strongest Banking Brand, 01 February 2021. https://brandfinance.com/press-releases/brand-finance-banking-500-2021-sber-named-worlds-strongest-banking-brand

Marvel Entertainment Inc. being one of the best-known examples:

Marvel Entertainment

Marvel's commercial strategy is based almost entirely on intangible assets, with 8,000 characters in the Marvel library delivering revenue via a series of licensing agreements distributing these characters beyond comic books to multiple media formats, including television, movies, and games.

CONCLUSION

Ideas are a product of your intellect, and the intellectual property facets of your idea are intangible assets – you can: keep, bequeath, and commercialize them.

Your ideas have value, which can be realised through the transition of *The Idea Lifecycle*™ four-step process:

1. **Ideation**
2. **Protection**
3. **Valuation**
4. **Sale**

That said, it isn't necessary for you as the creator to take the idea from conception to sale because ideas deliver monetary value at two stages – once they are registered as intellectual property, and secondly, when they are executed and produced.

While your ideas exist first and foremost in your mind, you are only able to protect them once they are transformed into a fixed and tangible medium. Once this happens, you can identify the intellectual property attributes and register them for legal protection under the relevant legal regime – copyright, patent, trademark, trade secret, and design mark law.

At its core, valuation of your intangible assets relies on the ability to legally register and control them to generate benefits, which can significantly increase the market value of your business. This may be done via brand marks, designs, inventions, proprietary technical, financial, marketing trade secrets, and know-how, which are often the key source of competitive advantage.

Even though intangible asset valuation is highly subjective, the use of cost, market, and future income models provide fundamental methods for estimating value.

However, the real value of intellectual property is the way in which you can commercialise your ideas as an integral part of your business: marketing, selling, capital raising, and brand building. Outright sale delivers a lump sum revenue inflow, whereas licensing gives you the opportunity to generate recurring revenue from your intangible assets whilst maintaining control over how they are used.

Ideas and innovations are your secret sauce and the key to your success.

Follow *The Ideas Lifecycle*™ and register your legal rights. . .

DON'T GIVE YOUR IDEAS AWAY FOR FREE!

About Kathryn

Kathryn Williams is the founder of KMint financial and pricing consultancy. Kathryn is the go-to finance guru for peak industry bodies, innovative and creative agencies around the world.

An internationally experienced consultant, mentor, workshop facilitator, keynote speaker, and author – Kathryn liaises closely with industry councils, is an Effie judge, is involved in benchmark studies, and is the author of several professional development booklets and host of the *KMint Asset Creation & Revenue Generation* webinar series.

As CFO consultant and mentor, Kathryn works with a multitude of agencies, from small independent agencies to global network leaders, resulting in deep expertise as to how the industry is really performing. Agency leaders engage Kathryn to fast-track financial efficiencies and effectiveness – taking advantage of the KMint Budget/Rolling Forecast Program, Rate Card and Revenue Calculator, End of Month Management Reporting Program, and Staff Career Matrix and KPI Scheme.

Creator of the signature workshop: *Show Me The Money*® and keynote *The Money Wheel*®, Kathryn is a passionate spokesperson about the commercialisation of creative ideas and services. Her keynote and workshop events inspire teams to understand the numbers that matter, giving them a competitive advantage – leading to overall agency profitability and holistic growth.

Kathryn studied Intellectual Property at Harvard University and was awarded top grading for her scholarly paper entitled Trademark – Who is entitled to benefit; and she is author of *Sell Your Ideas - How to value, protect and profit from your IP* – the guide for innovators, entrepreneurs, and creatives.

Learn how Kathryn can help you at:
- www.kathrynwilliams.com.au
- www.kmint.com.au
- www.showmethemoney.com.au

CHAPTER 6

CREATING YOUR CELEBRITY BRAND LOGLINE
HOW TO POSITION YOURSELF FOR SUCCESS

BY NICK NANTON & JW DICKS

So the head of the hip, cutting-edge ad agency was stymied. His client was just beginning to turn around his company's staid image – and was counting on the agency's new group of TV spots to complete its return to greatness.

And the head of the agency was very pleased with the work his creative team had done. He knew the spots would break through the clutter and deliver the message the company desperately *needed* to deliver.

The only problem was that the agency couldn't think of what *words* to use to deliver that message. It had to be a catchy, simple slogan that brought together all the different commercials with a powerful unifying vision.

Now, it was almost midnight and the agency head was beginning to panic. They had to have the slogan in place tomorrow to show the client. So he paced around at home trying to think of something – *anything* – that might work.

And for some reason Norman Mailer came to mind.

He had recently read Mailer's Pulitzer Prize-winning book, *The Executioner's Song* about the murderer Gary Gilmore, who Mailer had gotten to know when the convict was on death row. And he suddenly remembered what Gilmore's last words were before they flicked on the switch of the electric chair where he was seated.

"Let's do it," Gilmore had said.

The agency head remembered those words and how brave they had seemed to him, even coming from the mouth of a ruthless killer. It was a strong statement. And it seemed to him like it was exactly the kind of statement they needed.

But "Let's" was wrong. Everything wasn't a group activity. It should be "Just." *"Just do it."*

He thought that just might work for Nike.

Believe it or not, the above is a totally true story. Dan Wieden, one of the partners in the innovative Wieden + Kennedy ad agency (the ad agency's work propelled Nike to be named "Advertiser of the Year" twice at the Cannes Film Festival, the only company ever to have that honor), was completely stuck for a Nike slogan – until he remembered Gary Gilmore's last words.

SUMMING YOURSELF UP FOR SUCCESS

Even though the words came from a very unusual source, "Just Do It," of course, became one of the most well-known advertising slogans of the past few decades. Trying to sum up the appeal of a brand can be very tricky, difficult business; even though you only need to come up with a few words, they have to be the *right* words in order to convey the uniqueness of your brand to your existing customers and, more importantly, potential leads.

One of the first steps in the powerful process that we call 'StorySelling' (a topic that's the basis for a book we've written) is to do what Nike did – and find the right words to define your brand. We believe you do that by creating your "logline."

If you don't know what a logline is, it's a short one-to-three sentence encapsulation of the plot of a movie or TV show that's used to quickly sum it up – a little longer than an advertising tagline like "Let's Do It," but just as vital in defining what your Celebrity Brand is all about.

If you ever visit the movie and television indexing site, IMDB. com, you'll find millions of examples of loglines. Here are a couple of examples:

1. The CBS comedy: *2 Broke Girls*: "Two young women waitressing at a greasy spoon diner strike up an unlikely friendship in the hopes of launching a successful business – if only they can raise the cash."
2. The Leonardo DiCaprio thriller, *Inception*: "In a world where technology exists to enter the human mind through dream invasion, a highly-skilled thief is given a final chance at redemption which involves executing his toughest job to date: Inception."

As you can see in both of the above cases, a logline defines the main character(s), the situation, and the challenge. You need to do something similar with your logline to attract customers to who you are and what you're all about.

THE OBITUARY TEST

So, how do you go about figuring out what the right logline is for your brand? Don't worry, we're here to help.

We've discovered an incredibly useful exercise that will help you narrow your story down to its most important elements; it was created by author Klaus Fog, and it's called "The Obituary Test."[1] It's best summed up by the lyrics in Joni Mitchell's classic song, "Big Yellow Taxi" – *"You don't know what you've got 'til it's gone."*

In other words, what would your clients and customers miss the most about you if you were suddenly no longer around? By considering what your absence would mean to the people who buy from you, you can more easily uncover what's important about your story – because you're forced to identify what elements are the most crucial and compelling about your personal brand. This, in turn, helps you immensely in creating your StorySelling logline.

The exercise itself is simple – just write your "obituary," as if you were no longer with us (maybe get somebody to send you flowers to put you in the mood). As you do so, keep in mind the following questions:

- What's the biggest thing your business will be remembered for?
- What about the way you ran your business will be the most missed?
- Which customers will miss you the most and why?
- How were you different from others in the same business as you?

Most importantly, be *honest and factual* when you write your obituary – only write what your customers and clients

---

1. Klaus Fog, Storytelling: Branding in Practice, (Springer Heidelberg Dordrecht 2010), p. 72

would actually know and remember about you. And don't be embarrassed – nobody else has to see it except you (although it would be great if you shared it with people you trust and who know you well, to get their honest reactions).

You should also put some effort into creating the correct *headline* for your obituary – the first thing customers would write about you, based on your professional image. Because *that* is going to be your "Just Do It" moment.

And after you're done…we want you to write that obituary *again.*

Don't groan, this is our own twist on The Obituary Test and we think it's really the key to making it work – because this time, we want you to write your obituary the way YOU would like it to read. In other words, *don't* write it based on how your customers currently perceive you – but, instead, based on how you *want* to be perceived by them.

Let's use some make-believe obituary headlines as an example of what we're talking about. Let's say you're an investment consultant…and maybe, if your obit. was printed today, it might read:

LOCAL FINANCIAL PLANNER DIES; SERVED CLIENTS FOR 23 YEARS

But maybe you'd like it to read…

LOCAL FINANCIAL PLANNER SAFEGUARDED AND GREW CLIENTS' FORTUNES FOR DECADES

You can see the difference. The first headline is just a description; the second headline *tells* a story.

Here are a few other examples of obituary headlines that would reflect a lifetime of successful StorySelling:

CEO BATTLED CHILDHOOD POVERTY TO BUILD SUCCESSFUL BUSINESS

-——<<O>>-—-

INTERNET MARKETER MADE CLIENTS INTO MILLIONAIRES

-——<<O>>-—-

INNOVATIVE DENTIST USED CUTTING-EDGE TECHNOLOGY TO HELP PATIENTS

-——<<O>>-—-

REAL ESTATE AGENT'S CHARITY WORK BONDED HER TO COMMUNITY AND CLIENTS

You see what we mean? These headlines differentiate their subjects and make them *more* than just another professional. They're known for something *specific* and *beneficial* that they accomplish.

So go ahead. Work on that second obituary. When you're done, go back and take a look at the first one you wrote and compare it with your sec- ond one. If they're pretty similar, you're in good shape; if they're very different, however, you're looking at the distance that StorySelling will need to transport your Celebrity Brand.

Now, many of you may have had difficulty coming up with that second obit. You weren't sure what to write – or aren't happy with what you ended up writing. That's not unusual. If you are having trouble coming up with your logline, let's drill a little deeper and see if we strike oil.

DEVELOPING YOUR LOGLINE

Your logline can focus on one of several different aspects of your per- sonal and professional life, depending on what works

74

best for your Celebrity Brand. In this section, we're going to ask you some questions – six of them to be exact. Your answers will hopefully help you identify the key points that make you stand out – and that will attract others to your story.

- **Question 1: What have you done?**

Personal stories of overcoming hardship and/or outstanding accomplishment are always valuable to a Celebrity Brand.

Fans of the legendary motivational speaker and author Zig Ziglar, who passed away in 2012, knew and loved his personal story: the 10th of 11 children whose father died when he was six, and only realized his potential when a supervisor motivated him to greatness in his salesman job.

Similarly, Dan Kennedy, a direct marketing legend, has exploited his background as a copywriting genius who took on the advertising establishment with his famous "No B.S." approach. He tells his "herd" that he's the living proof that there's more than one way to sell successfully.

And, by the way, some people use elements of their backgrounds that don't really have anything at all to do with their current professions. For example, one of our clients is a real estate investment expert in Canada who used to be a policeman; he now positions himself as "The Wealthy Cop," in spite of the fact that law enforcement has precious little to do with buying and selling homes. It doesn't matter though – because people (a) remember who he is because of that nickname and (b) trust him more because he was a policeman.

- **Question #2: Who are you?**

We're looking for more than your name here – we're looking for personal qualities you possess that make you stand out from others *like* you.

Think of President Ronald Reagan's old nickname – "The Great Communicator." His "brand" was his ability to convey complex information in simple terms everyone could understand and relate to. Think of legendary soul singer James Brown's designation as "The Hardest Working Man in Show Business" – meaning you knew that when you went to see his show, you would see a *show*.

So, what about you makes you distinct? And, remember, it could be as simple as something you wear – remember Larry King and his suspenders night after night?

• Question #3: What's your title?

When Michael Jackson was at his peak, MTV desperately wanted to have him on an awards show. He said, "Sure – if you agree to call me 'The King of Pop' every time you refer to me." MTV shrugged and said, "Whatever" – they didn't care, as long as he showed. Result? People began to call him "The King of Pop" everywhere he appeared, and that's how he was referred to in the press when he died.

Even though it's a title he created for himself!

So, we guess, the real question here shouldn't be: "What's your title?" but "What do you want your title to be?" If it actually fits your situation, as it did with Jackson, you can make it stick. Another one of our clients, Richard Seppala, helps small companies realize more money from their marketing, so he calls himself "The ROI Guy." That's his title and that's how people remember him.

• Question #4: How is your product or service different?

Another compelling logline you may be able to write could have to do with an innovative product or service that sets you apart from the competition. For instance, we know who Colonel Sanders was because his KFC chain used his "top-secret" chicken recipe to StorySell their authenticity and food quality; similarly, entrepreneur Wally Amos used his personality and his delicious cookie recipe to StorySell his "Famous Amos" cookie line. And what's interesting about both men is that they both sold out to other companies who continued to StorySell them even after they were no longer involved!

So how is your product or service different? Is it faster? (Think of the 5 Minute Car Wash.) Is it for you? (Burger King is "Be Your Way," after all.) Is it changing with the times? ("It's not TV. It's – Oops! Something went wrong. Try restarting your HBO Max app.") If it really stands out, you're the person who made it stand out – and that makes you more impressive in your logline.

- **Question #5: What's your attitude?**

In 1911, Thomas Watson was tired of sitting through uninspiring business meetings – so one day, he just got up, walked over to the easel and wrote the word "THINK" in big letters on the paper. Three years later, when he started IBM, he remembered that moment and made that word a single word slogan that is still used to represent the business machine giant today (their company magazine was called *Think*).

Almost a century later, when Steve Jobs was ready to take over Apple again in 1997, he wanted a similar impactful statement to define his company – so he launched a multi-million dollar campaign around two words: "Think Different." Many saw it as a direct response to IBM's one word.

Whatever the case, both men used their basic philosophy – *or attitude* – as the underpinning for their loglines. Even Nike's modified Gary Gilmore line, "Just Do It," is all about attitude. Maybe your particular approach makes you memorable – if so, tap into it.

- **Question #6: What do you promise?**

FedEx pledges that they'll deliver to "The World on Time." The U.S. Postal Service, in contrast, says, "If It Fits, It Ships." Meanwhile, UPS insists that nobody's better than they are as "United Problem Solvers." Three different delivery systems all focusing on different benefits or promises.

Many successful brands and businesses have been built on promises – such as the Domino's Pizza chain, with their guarantee that deliveries would come in "30 Minutes or Less" and Wal-Mart with "Save money. Live Better."

So, what promise can you (or do you) consistently deliver on? Is it strong enough to be a part of your logline?

These are the main crucial areas you can explore to create your own logline. Some of these areas overlap and you may end up tapping into more than one of them for your final composition (as long as you keep it simple!).

Again, only you can decide what is the right logline for your StorySelling narrative. Again, however, it's useful to do a reality check by showing your choice to friends and associates, as well as any branding consultants you might employ, to ensure your logline is both authentic and impactful. Remember, just because it works for you doesn't necessarily mean it will work for your customers, so feedback is essential.

Once you've decided on your logline, consider it the foundation of your "brand story." Use it in some fashion in everything you do from a marketing perspective. Legends like Richard Branson and Warren Buffett always make sure that everything they do represents their brand; it helps them to continue to convert every new undertaking into a success.

So why shouldn't you?

About Nick

From the slums of Port-au-Prince, Haiti with special forces raiding a sex trafficking ring and freeing children; to the Virgin Galactic Space Port in Mojave with Sir Richard Branson, Nick is passionate about telling stories that connect.

He has directed more than 60 documentaries and a sold-out Broadway Show (garnering 43 Emmy nominations in multiple regional and national competitions, and 22 wins). He has made films and shows featuring: Larry King, Jack Nicklaus, Tony Robbins, Sir Richard Branson, Dean Kamen, Lisa Nichols, Peter Diamandis and many more. He is currently the host of *In Case You Didn't Know...with Nick Nanton* on Amazon Prime, and regularly hosts the podcast *Now to Next with Nick Nanton* which can be found on all popular podcast platforms.

Nick also enjoys serving as an Elder at Orangewood Church, supporting Young Life, Entrepreneurs International and rooting for the Florida Gators with his wife Kristina and their three children, Brock, Bowen and Addison.

Learn more at:
- www.NickNanton.com
- www.CelebrityBrandingAgency.com
- www.DNAmedia.com

About JW

JW Dicks, Esq., is the CEO of DN Agency, an Inc. 5000 Multimedia Company that represents over 3,000 clients in 63 countries.

He is a *Wall Street Journal* Best-Selling Author® who has authored or co-authored over 47 books, a 7-time Emmy® Award-winning Executive Producer and a Broadway Show Producer.

JW is an Ansari XPRIZE Innovation Board member, Chairman of the Board of the National Retirement Council™, Chairman of the Board of the National Academy of Best-Selling Authors®, Board Member of the National Association of Experts, Writers and Speakers®, and a Board Member of the International Academy of Film Makers®.

He has been quoted on business and financial topics in national media such as *USA Today, The Wall Street Journal, Newsweek, Forbes, CNBC.com,* and *Fortune Magazine Small Business.*

JW has co-authored books with legends like Jack Canfield, Brian Tracy, Tom Hopkins, Dr. Nido Qubein, Steve Forbes, Richard Branson, Michael Gerber, Dr. Ivan Misner, and Dan Kennedy.

JW has appeared and interviewed on business television shows airing on ABC, NBC, CBS, and FOX affiliates around the country and co-produces and syndicates a line of franchised business television shows such as *Success Today, Wall Street Today, Hollywood Live,* and *Profiles of Success.*

JW and his wife of 47 years, Linda, have two daughters, and four granddaughters. He is a sixth-generation Floridian and splits his time between his home in Orlando and his beach house on Florida's west coast.

CHAPTER 7

SUCCESS IS A #$@#^% WORD!
YOUR PRACTICAL GUIDE TO FREEDOM

BY MEGA R. MEASE

My awareness of four-letter words began at the sweet age of four. It was evident in no uncertain terms that four-letter words were terrible, ugly, disrespectful, and should never be spoken! Of course, this didn't apply to me because I was just learning the alphabet. I didn't even know or care what these words were! It was different for my older sibling, who was constantly in trouble for breaking this all-important family rule. I never heard what words she was punished for speaking; however, I saw the consequences for saying them. What to do? How could I not say them if I didn't know what they were?

You may be asking yourself, what does this have to do with Success? Chances are when drawn to Cracking the Code to anything, especially Success, failure has most likely been experienced in at least one endeavor or perhaps many. I invite you to read on and find yourself in my adventure, a lovely yet rocky road to attaining and sustaining Success in multiple areas of my life.

Things began to make sense when I was able to read words and short sentences. I was taught to read and write four-letter words; Love, Good, This, That, and my favorite, Hero! None of them were terrible, so what were those unspeakable words? The more they were hidden, the more curious I became.

There is always wisdom as we grow older, and I hit the jackpot at six years old:

○ Don't...
○ Can't...
○ Won't...
○ Stop...
○ Quit...
○ Lazy...
○ Busy...

Standing by themselves, these words stuck out; however, they could instantly stunt creativity and imagination when used in a sentence and even stop us in their tracks.

— **"Don't** do that."
— "You **can't** do that."
— "You **won't** get far with that attitude."
— **"Stop** that right now!"
— **"Don't** be **lazy!"**
— "Only losers **quit!"**
— "I'm too **busy!"**

Of course, I soon figured out that these weren't the forbidden family words I'd been seeking. Luckily, my inquiring mind kept my curiosity alive! Instead, these words were subliminal messages, an array of four-letter words that had redirected my life and slowly crept in as they remodeled my identity. Unsuspecting, well-meaning parents, teachers, and other mentors had unintentionally contributed to stunting the pathways to my authentic life prosperity.

Decades later, it became distinctly apparent that Ms. Success was the Mother of those readily available and accepted four-letter words. She had masqueraded herself with those three extra letters. I had uncovered the secret that Success was a wolf in sheep's clothing, a front runner of #$@#^% words!

Children are often bombarded with so many different, subliminal definitions of Success that their pathway may become muddy. As adults, the many shades of Success undoubtedly silently birth an array of questions resulting in reactions of fear, unworthiness, confusion, overwhelm, and therefore eventually becoming stuck without knowing it. The one constant and saving grace is that one shoe doesn't fit all.

Undeniably, I was in the company of many others whose pathways had been altered as well. Again, what to do? This time I knew the answer. Moving beyond the often-unintended damage meant finding another avenue, or better yet, an Expressway to Fullness of Self.

The beginnings of Cracking the Code to Success are harvested from this baseline. It's no secret that we live what we learn. Each teaching has a positive and negative pole. The tricky and sometimes overlooked piece of the equation is the balance of contrary forces, the Yin and Yang. A positive pole also has a negative component. Likewise, the negative pole has a positive component. The challenge is finding value in both while aligning ourselves with our personal integrity.

This journey is distinctive and specific for each person, depending on their likes, dislikes, and life experiences. Thus, to Crack the Code of anything, one must begin with an open mind, self-awareness, lack of judgment, and often forgiveness. Returning to the source is where the answers have always been waiting to be found. Sounds simple, but how do we acquire those "must-haves"?

The good news is that a steadfast development of commitment is much more accessible than most think. Observation shows that our lives are enhanced when we include positive thoughts and words in our daily actions. Improved outlook and attitude, forward movement thinking reduces stress and improves our health, relationships, self-esteem, and overall Success in life.

Your beliefs become your thoughts,
Your thoughts become your words,
Your words become your actions,
Your actions become your habits,
Your habits become your values,
Your values become your destiny.
~ Mahatma Gandhi

Interestingly, a mathematical theory called local and global maximum is an ideal doorway into understanding the map of simplicity and attaining Success in all areas of life. Understandably, our human self wants to enjoy life at the highest point, live at an optimal level, and achieve our maximum potential in all areas, all of the time. This goal lives under the roof of the global maximum. While attainable, the prep work is massive, takes much time, and includes extensive study of self-awareness. It's easy to get stuck in the goal's enormity and, therefore, move in circles. The local maximum concept supports us in understanding our humanness and busy minds. It teaches us to begin with small, conscious decisions, which in time manifest Success in ways better than we ever imagined!

ENERGETIC VIBRANCY, BALANCE, AND SUCCESS ARE POSSIBLE!

Everything is energy, so it makes sense to first connect with the source when setting out to accomplish a task of any size. Attaining Success doesn't have to be a long, grueling, painful journey. Instead, by addressing life energetically, much of the harmful stress evaporates. The road to Success is less cluttered and therefore simplified.

Time is a finite and valuable resource. However, while working to arrive at the top of the Success ladder, time needs to be put into perspective. Why? Very often, the target goal leads to longer hours, disappointment, and inevitably burnout. Energy is different in that it is palatable and measurable in productivity. Our intensity of energy on many levels significantly increases our capacity to get things done efficiently and quickly.

There is no better way to live a complete and balanced life than beginning with self. A healthy mind, body, and spirit lead to Success. I do not know where the following healing hand exercises originated. I can say that they are simple, easy, quick and they work. I invite you to enjoy them and witness how your Successes grow.

ACTION ONE: Heart-Centered Breathing!

One love, one heart, one destiny.
~ Robert Marley

The heart knows best, and this exercise confirms it. HCB is an easy practice that beautifully draws the head energy and heart energy together. It keeps our consciousness engaged in a healthy flow while supporting the attainment of growth without the normal human resistance. Enjoy this calming meditation while sitting, laying down, or standing. It's sublime to begin and end your day with this mudra.

Place hands flat over the heart center, located in the middle of the chest between the breasts. Breathe slowly, deeply, and with ease. Sense one movement of the energy swinging from the front of the heart center to the back of the body. Repeat this with each breath. A sense of "true calm" usually generates within a minimum of 3 – 5 minutes. Do this anywhere at any time. Try it because it just feels so good!

ACTION TWO: Know, Flow, and GO

If you feel that you are going without, go within.

~ Rasheed Ogunlaru

The upside (Yang) of operating in "autopilot" mode allows one to accomplish tasks quickly and correctly without thinking. The Yin side includes boredom created by not being fully conscious in decision-making, which invisibly fuels a lack of movement. Invariably, Success is either slowed down or altogether eliminated.

Preparation: Have fun acknowledging both your conscious and autopilot actions. Watch yourself for a full day and notice all your mundane movements and routines. Make a list of seven actions you do daily and are willing to change just a wee bit. Keep in mind that these are not significant changes or goals. Instead, they are actions that we don't often ponder.

Time to brainstorm! Make a list of the changes you are going to embrace for each of the seven days. Each day add your next Know-Flow-Go to your daily actions. By Day seven, you will be enjoying your entire list of changes every day.

Examples:

- **Day 1:** I brush my top teeth first.
- **K-F-G**: I will brush my bottom teeth first.

- **Day 2:** I put both socks on first and then my shoes.
- K-F-G: I will put a sock and shoe on first. Then do the same on the other foot.

- **Day 3:** I take the same route to work every day.
- K-F-G: I will take a different route as I drive to work.

- **Day 4:** I have slept on the same side of the bed for years.
- **K-F-G:** I will sleep on the other side of the bed.

- **Day 5:** I check my email as soon as I wake up.
- **K-F-G:** I will eat breakfast before I check email.

- **Day 6:** I watch the news on the same channel every day.
- **K-F-G:** I will watch a different news channel.

- **Day 7:** I drive off before I see the garage door completely closed.
- **K-F-G:** I will wait to make sure that the garage door is closed.

- **Day 8-30:** Continue embracing all seven changes daily.

- **Day 31:** Look back and notice the beginnings of the new, improved you as you propel yourself to new heights of Success.

ACTION THREE: GUIDANCE

Expect abundance to receive abundance.
~ Debasish Mridha

Energy and blessings are received into the palms of our hands. Focusing our eyes on them sends healing power to our minds. Performing this simple mudra opens energetic pathways enabling us to receive guidance without words! Performing this mudra over time encourages enhanced intuition and knowing. Our hands, arms, and shoulders are directly connected to the heart center chakra. While not necessary to reap the benefits, daily practice often results in feeling the hands being filled up. Lasting results may be experienced by performing the mudra alone. Heart-Centered Breathing, however, before or afterward encourages a more profound knowledge of the guidance given.

Sit with your spine straight. Place hands comfortably in front of your chest, palms up with the sides of the little fingers touching. Leave a tiny opening between the sides of the little fingers. Ask for guidance on a particular issue, problem, goal, vision, or general direction with nothing in mind. With your neck straight, focus your eyes at the tip of your nose and toward the palms. Breathe slow, deep, long, and mindfully into your palms. Allow yourself to feel the hands becoming heavy as they fill with the vibration of the guidance you seek. Smile intermittently to support the body to relax and receive.

ACTION FOUR: HAPPINESS

The happiness of your life depends upon the quality
of your thoughts.
~ Marcus Aurelius

Happiness does not have to be dependent upon circumstances. It's a choice to make a conscious effort daily to be the best we can be and appreciate life. Commit to being happy at this moment, this day, the next day, and all the days afterward! Practice this mudra regularly, and you will find yourself in a more joyful place, regardless of any pitfalls that may occur.

Sit comfortably with spine straight and elbows lifted to the side and away from the body. Curl the small and ring fingers so that they are touching the palms. Gently hold them in place with your thumbs. The other two fingers will point straight up. Take long, deep, controlled breaths while focusing on the third eye.

Don't Worry – Be Happy! Doing this when you already feel happy anchors the feeling in your system, which supports choosing to be happy more often. The domino effect is feeling engaged, productive, and satisfied with all the tiny successes achieved on your way to the granddaddy of Success that was your goal.

ACTION FIVE: FEARLESS

There is only one thing that makes a dream impossible to achieve:
the fear of failure.
~ Paulo Coelho

A critical factor in attaining Success is to walk through fear with mindfulness. The Fearless Mudra supports us in energetically embracing fear with focus. Doing this mudra before fear shows its ugly head can spare us much pain and suffering.

Place one hand in front of the navel with the palm facing upward. Raise the right arm with the hand at shoulder height. The palm will be facing forward with fingers and thumbs straight up. Concentrate on the Third Eye chakra located in the middle of the forehead. Take deep, mindful, slow breaths as you consciously embrace your fears.

ACTION SIX: CHARGE YOUR BATTERY

Think about every good thing in your life right now. Free yourself from worrying. Let go of the anxiety, breathe. Stay positive.
~ Germany Kent

Sit comfortably with your back straight. Take a couple of deep breaths. Smile as you let go. Put your arms out straight out in front of your body. Make a fist with the right hand. Take another breath. The fingers of your left hand will wrap around your right hand. Make sure that the palms are touching. Next, place your thumbs close together and point them up. Soften your shoulders. For several minutes take deep, controlled breaths as you focus on your thumbs. Take note of your calm!

I shall end with the wisdom of Brian Tracy:

Imagine no limitations; decide what's right and desirable before you decide what's possible.

Once the answers you seek are discovered, jump on your Expressway, and apply them to any situation, problem, or my personal favorite, your dream of attaining the best life imaginable.

About Mega

Mega R. Mease, known as the "Everyday Ordinary Healer," is a Holistic Health Entrepreneur and founder/ owner of the Center for Advanced Energy Therapeutics and the CAET Community Wellness Volunteer Program in Tucson, Arizona. Additionally, she is on the Board of the National Alliance of Energy Practitioners. Her passion is providing a vehicle in which others learn to live a happier, healthier existence.

She describes her pathway to success as a long, sometimes treacherous, and yet exciting winding road. Her work evolved slowly and sometimes painfully out of her natural abilities and life circumstances rather than clear-cut goals that were mindfully planned. Therefore, she sees her work as a life "calling" rather than a sought-after career.

When asked, "Who are you and what do you do?" she answers with an ear-to-ear grin: "Today, I am fully engaged in a life of joy, authenticity, and fulfillment. Holistic health isn't only a professional path; it's my lifestyle. Family and friends are my greatest treasures; my work is my play, and service is my nurture."

People of all walks of life and ages come to her seeking stress reduction, relaxation, and guidance. These include those with mental, emotional, and physical challenges as well as people with life-threatening diseases. Her rare deep-seated wisdom regarding manifestation can be experienced in the energy healing, health, wealth, relationship, and business arenas. Mega refers to her credentials as simply fancy words that attempt to describe how she spends her time. In her words...

"I earn my keep here on earth by supporting others on their path to empowerment and joy."

Mega's skillsets as an Energy Healer and Energy Diagnostician are utilized in all of the services she provides. The foundation is seeing and finding the emotional trauma in the physical body and auric field that is sourced by illness, disease, disorder, depression, grief, and other forms of crises. The value of her work continues with the energy movement that holds the condition in place.

Several healing methods have been birthed from Mega's decades of experience. Her longstanding involvement in Energy Healing, Nutrition, and Self–Empowerment led to the creation and development of HeartRay™ Energetic Therapy, Bone Energy Re-Pattering™, FootFlex™, and the Mega Method™ of Healing. Staying true to her Reiki roots, Mega lives, loves, and walks the Reiki path and therefore utilizes it as the foundation of the more invasive methods she has created.

Last but not least, Ms. Mease is credited with building, directing, and funding the longest-standing Hospital Reiki Volunteer Program in the United States from 2006-2016. Over 7,000 Reiki sessions were provided by Mega and her staff. Now, renamed and relocated to the Center, The CAET Community Wellness Volunteer Program offers an array of holistic services provided by several practitioners free of charge. Recipients must be under the care of a physician and being treated for cancer, on a transplant list, diagnosed with a brain injury, or be a veteran struggling with PTSD and other anxiety-based challenges

The majority of Mega's services are available both in-house and remotely.

Reach out today:
- www.AdvancedEnergyTherapeutics.com
- www.megaRmease.com
- www.facebook.com/groups/Abundance

CHAPTER 8

SUCCESS IS THE NATURAL OUTCOME OF GREAT TEAMWORK

BY MICHAEL REZA

Never doubt that a small group of thoughtful, committed people can change the world. Indeed, it is the only thing that ever has.
~ Margaret Mead

As human beings, we can only see the arc of our lives in retrospect. When I look back from where I stand now, I am in awe of how blessed my life has been from the very beginning. I was born into a family that believed in the power of teamwork. Our family functioned like a well-oiled machine. In fact, we were the definition of teamwork as defined by Webster's Dictionary: *joint action by a group, in which each person subordinates her or his individual interests and opinions to the unity and efficiency of the group.* For example, Dad was a Navy man, and with eight kids, it was like the movie *Yours, Mine and Ours.* We had schedules and chores, and my favorite – two-minute showers – that went like this. We had to wet ourselves down, turn the water off, scrub-a-dub-dub, turn the water back on, rinse off, and done! Then we would yell, "next"!

Our family, while not wealthy, was rich in unconditional love, and we were comfortable. My parents were Christians – my 90-year-old dad still is – and it was the values, principles, and love of the Divine which they instilled in their kids, weaving this love into every aspect of our lives.

As the eldest of eight children, I took to the concept of teamwork naturally, and I took my role as oldest son seriously. Very early on, I learned that there were responsibilities that came along with being a team member and being the oldest. It was my responsibility to set a good example for my younger brothers and sisters. This gave my life purpose, and at the time, I had no idea how that purpose would serve to develop competence and confidence, both qualities which are necessary to the cultivation of a successful life. I have to say it was the very notion of teamwork that made me realize our oneness with everything in life and how, when the team runs smoothly, everything runs smoothly.

As far as I knew, when I was a young boy, all families worked the same way – as a team. Of course, I eventually found out that other families did not function the way ours did, but that had absolutely no bearing on my outlook on life. In school, I joined every sports team that I could. That was the way I lived – starting in grade school into high school and through college,

I was part of many teams. What I loved was that even though each person on the team did their individual best, which was always acknowledged, the success of the team was paramount. Every team I became part of was led by inspiring coaches who served to deepen my commitment to being a team player. This has been my experience time and time again throughout my life: success is a natural outcome of any team with a good leader. As Michael Jordan once said, "Talent wins games, but teamwork wins championships."

A BRIEF EYE-OPENING DETOUR
AWAY FROM THE TEAM

Alone we can do so little; together we can do so much.
~ Helen Keller

I have to chuckle when I recall my one brief experience attempting to do something solo; even I had to stray a little. Fortunately, it was a short-lived venture, and it happened when I was in my late teens. Here's what happened. We lived in Southern California, near Los Angeles. It was difficult not to be influenced by the creative aspects of life being expressed all around me. We were surrounded by great displays of wealth and all sorts of creative people. There were famous and not-so-famous actors and musicians, singers and directors, producers and writers everywhere. For a while, I fancied myself joining the stellar ranks of those in the creative limelight.

I started writing songs at first, then jingles, and did a little production work. It felt good to produce things on my own. I wrote a song inspired by my love of God and the Divine. I was especially proud of this song that I called *Heavenly Desire*. I ended up selling the rights to this song to a publisher and just knew it was going to be a big hit! I could see my life as a creative genius unfolding. Well, nothing of the sort happened. One day I found out that my wonderful song was being used in a porno film!! I didn't understand how that could happen. It didn't take long to figure it out, though. The fact is, I was working on my own. And, when you sell the creative rights to something, you no longer have any say in how or where that creative expression will be used. Right then and there, I decided I wanted to know how my efforts were going to affect others. I was disenchanted with working on my own, and I was inspired to go in a different direction.

FINDING THE RIGHT TEAM

*Coming together is a beginning, staying together is progress,
and working together is success.*
~ Henry Ford

I wasn't sure what I wanted to do after I gave up my creative career. But I didn't have to think about it too long. Another door opened almost immediately. A friend's brother offered me a job in his mortgage business. I accepted and went to work learning all about the lending business. The first time I helped a young couple buy a home, I was captured hook, line and sinker.

The story of this young family touched my heart. They had a newborn with health issues and wanted to be able to bring their baby to their own home where the child would have its own room instead of the small apartment where they currently lived. Helping this young family become homeowners, seeing the joy and happiness they felt was indescribable. I'm not sure who felt more elated, them or me! Honestly, when I handed them the keys to their new home, the sense of fulfillment almost overwhelmed me. Right then and there, I made a commitment to work in the financial industry as a lender in order to be able to help people. I felt like I was in a field I could call home.

A PASSION TO GIVE AND TO HELP OTHERS REIGNITES AND OPENS MANY DOORS

My very first experience in lending reignited a passion within me for helping others. I was reminded of how wonderful it felt when I helped my brothers and sisters with their homework. They all looked up to me, and I have to say, I loved the feeling. I felt important and essential to the family team. As a member of a fine lending team, I knew I could play an important role in the lives of so many people helping them buy homes. Once this passion flared up, it has never diminished.

Helping others as part of a team has been my life since that early experience. When I was still working at the mortgage company, I also helped two of my siblings go back to school and get their degrees. Their diligence and commitment served to inspire me to go back to school to get my MBA.

THE DOORS KEPT OPENING TO BE OF GREATER HELP

After making the commitment to serve through lending and went back to school for my MBA, the doors literally started swinging open, one after another. I met powerful and passionate people in high places. As a result of the work we were doing at the mortgage company Fannie Mae tapped us and we became the largest lender to Native Americans. In addition, we were part of the team that created public policy in the way of credit scoring that standardized a way of approving loans that eliminated discriminatory acts. This allows more honest, hard-working people to get approved for home loans.

Back in 1982, I was also appointed and confirmed by Congress to become part of the team that created the Congressional Awards Act here in the U.S. This concept was founded in Europe by Prince Phillip, the Duke of Edinburgh, for the purposes of acknowledging youth in service. As a non-partisan bill, Congress voted the Congressional Awards Act in without a hitch. It went on to become the most successful of all the programs around the world and still is to this day.

SUCCESS MEANS DIFFERENT THINGS TO DIFFERENT PEOPLE

Train up a child in the way he should go; and when he is old
he will not depart from it.
~ Proverbs 22:6

There is not a time in my life when I have not felt successful. Fortunately, my parents did not sow seeds of success vs. failure. Each and every one of the children was considered by our parents to be successful in that we had arrived on this planet as expressions of the Divine. That in and of itself was a great success. We were taught that finding work we love and, as I mentioned earlier, being part of a team in which we did our best and contributed to the team endeavor would always lead to success. The love and support of my parents, the support and camaraderie of teammates and colleagues have lifted me throughout my life.

Like so many people, my early ideas of success involved all the usual notions: lots of money, fancy cars, clothes, trips, and bling. There's absolutely nothing wrong with those ideas, but eventually, one comes to understand that those things are the icing on the cake. The cake is what provides the canvas for the icing. And everyone can decorate his or her cake with whatever they desire. Financial independence and all the good things life has to offer can certainly be indicative of a successful life.

THE MORE YOU GIVE, THE MORE YOU RECEIVE

To those who have, more will be given. From those who have little, even that will be taken.
~ Matthew 13:12

I love this quote from Matthew. I have learned that this statement is about how we think, our mindset. If you are always complaining about not having enough or not being successful enough, then you will always be wanting. If, on the other hand, you feel richly supplied and you share what you have with others, you will be given more.

Today my greatest pleasure is being able to share these concepts and the many gifts I've been given with others. I love to introduce my team members to travel. Each year I take my family along with the entire staff and their families on an exotic trip. Together my wife and I teach our four children the value of teamwork and pray that they will continue in their own ways to enjoy being a member of a team that contributes to the ever-evolving good.

To say that I am a staunch proponent of teamwork is an understatement. I have been driven by being part of exceptional teams my entire life. From grade school to the excellent high school I attended, and the great sports teams led by exceptional coaches to the universities I attended, I have been surrounded by individuals that embrace and revel in being on winning teams. Every company I have been privileged to join, I thought of as a team. Every business I started, I created like I was putting together a championship team. I simply cannot imagine not being part of a team. And I simply cannot imagine a life that is not successful when the concept of teamwork is embraced.

ESSENTIAL QUALITIES I'VE LEARNED ARE NECESSARY FOR SUCCESSFUL TEAMS

My life launched me directly into teamwork. From my perspective, there is no individual success. We cannot do anything without the help and support of others. We cannot make a family. We cannot create a business. Great inventions, while attributed to individuals, emerge out of teamwork. Einstein had to be fed. He was married and therefore part of a team. He was surrounded by intellectuals with whom he could discuss his ideas and theories. Likewise, artists cannot survive without the support of some kind of team effort. Books cannot be written, and movies cannot be made. Life is teamwork.

If you are in the stage of life where you are attempting to define success for yourself, think of opening your mind to the team concept. If you've been struggling, trying to achieve some form of individual success, perhaps it's time to re-evaluate and look at how you can contribute more as a team player. As part of a team, you may just find a different definition of success.

The following qualities are those I find essential to being part of any team:

- Trust: First of all is trust. Trusting in something greater than oneself.
- Acceptance of accountability: Each team member must take 100% responsibility for their actions and do their very best.
- Support one another: Under any and all circumstances, encourage and support your teammates.
- Pride in the collective work of the team: Be proud of what your team accomplishes.

As a team leader or a coach, it's essential to create the conditions and atmosphere in which team members will thrive and in which the team will experience success. I've compiled these attributes over the course of my time as a team member and now, as the owner of my own company, continuously striving to further the advancement of the team.

A leader must always motivate and inspire team members, helping them feel supported and valued. A leader must have a clear vision for the team and have an understanding and acceptance of each person's roles and responsibilities. A leader is not seeking personal credit and glory. This takes inner security which, when displayed, inspires team members to follow suit. A leader also encourages the free flow of ideas and opinions without judging the person and letting others know it's okay to disagree.

In my experience, when you are part of an inspired and inspiring team, success is already yours.

I am not alone in my opinion about teamwork and success. I leave you with another of my favorite quotes, an African proverb that sums it up so clearly:

If you want to go fast, go alone. If you want to go far, go together.

About Michael

Distinguished in several professional arenas, Michael Reza's name is synonymous with fair lending practices in the financial industry, fair representation of his constituents in politics, as the long-term Congressional Awards President and Board Member, and as an Executive Producer in the film industry. He also actively participates in service to others through raising funds and awareness for a variety of organizations devoted to cancer research, youth, and HRH Prince Phillip Duke of Edinburgh's Award.

While serving on Fannie Mae's advisory board, Michael became the first lender entrusted to secure and issue mortgage-backed securities to Native Americans in the U.S.A. Michael has backed more than $50M worth of loans to this previously ignored population. Subsequently, through active participation in the first tax credit to Native Americans in the US, and after the sale of the tax credit, he went on to slash loan amounts and payments by 50%.

Michael was the President of the 34th Congressional District appointed by the local Congressman Esteban Torres. He was then appointed and confirmed to the Board of Directors of the Congressional Awards Board in 1993, for which Congress had to vet and vote him onto the Board. He was unanimously confirmed and approved by both, and he served in that role through 2003. [*N.B. The Congressional Award is the highest award given to youth in the U.S.A. and it was voted into Public Law 96-114.*]

In his early years in the financial industry, after earning his MBA, Michael started a mortgage company which he led for 20 years before selling it to a public company. He then started another mortgage banking division which was subsequently sold to HomeServices of America, a Berkshire Hathaway Affiliate recognized as the largest, full-service independent residential real estate brokerage firm and the largest brokerage-owned settlement services (mortgage, title, escrow, and insurance) provider in the United States.

As the CEO and an owner of MCapital, Michael continues to build and cultivate long-term quality relationships by consistently providing exceptional customer service. He currently sits as an advisor or board member on over

25 companies from banks to non-profits, and serves as Executive Producer on the TV show, *It's Happening Right Here.*

Michael is expanding his reach into new territory as co-author of *Cracking The Success Code Vol. 2*, with Brian Tracy and *The Soul of Success Vol. 2*, co-authored with Jack Canfield. All proceeds from these books are being donated to a variety of causes including non-profits that are leading the way to bring an end to human trafficking among others.

Michael lives in Southern California with his wife, their three teenage children and his oldest son, Miles Reza lives in Florida.

CHAPTER 9

HOW WE PASS ON OUR MONEY SAYS AN AWFUL LOT ABOUT OUR VALUES

BY GARY WOOLMAN

"Money makes the world go round, the world go round,
the world go round.
Money makes the world go round, it's such a happy sound."
~ Cabaret (movie)

Whether you are a fan of the movie *Cabaret* or not, chances are you are familiar with the lyrics from the movie's most popular song. The unobstructed, continuous flow of money is the basis of solid economies. It's what makes families feel secure and safe. It's what makes businesses successful.

I've experienced what happens to a family when the money stops flowing, and business isn't successful, and believe me, it is not a happy sound! As a result of this experience, I've devoted my life to understanding money, how it flows, what obstructs its flow, how to help family businesses improve their cash flow, and how to create a successful transition plan while de-risking business.

I've not pursued this path for the love of money. Rather, I've pursued it for the love of family and the legacy of safety and security that a family business can pass on to future generations. Additionally, I've pursued the financial path to prove that faith, combined with knowledge, is truly a powerful combination that can get anyone through the most challenging times. What our family experienced became the inspiration that set me on the path to my life's work and passion. This is integral to how I continue to help business owners to this very day.

———————

My dad was a hard-working, innovative, and upright man. He was a beloved coach who is still fondly remembered at the small Christian college where he was also a professor, Dean of Men, and Athletic Director. Eventually, he decided to leave the academic world and go into private business.

Dad joined a very successful business and was positioned as a limited partner with three general principals. The business manufactured oil and gas additives that more effectively prevented carbon build-up and cleaned fuel system components. It was designed to compete against the very popular STP brand. My dad was doing great, making more money than he had as a teacher and coach. Our family was living the high life. We had a big house and a big fancy car. I remember how proud I felt taking my date to the senior prom in our Lincoln Continental.

Soon after joining the company, dad "secured" a huge contract with the state of Kentucky transportation department, which I believe was the largest order his company had ever received. Based on the results of the initial trial with the product, the state approved and placed a $25 million pre-order with the condition to perform a final test of the product before the sale was finalized.

This was when the first problem was discovered. Before the test could be run, my dad had to ensure the inventory would be ready for timely delivery to the state of Kentucky. His company required him to personally secure a one million dollar loan based on the order. How he got this loan is still a mystery, but somehow, he was allowed to get that, and he was "off to the races." He viewed this as a no-risk deal! He was "sure" that he would be able to pay off the loan as soon as the order was approved and then paid for. Then the business and our family would be securely, happily, humming along.

However, the second problem surfaced, and this was the blow that took him to the mat. It turned out that one of the owners did not have the same high-minded and moral values which my dad lived by. In fact, this person was in the mafia and wanted to make a bigger profit by making a cheaper product. He told the chemists to change the formula, which they did, without consulting with or telling my dad. When dad found out about the formula change, he immediately told his contact person with the state of Kentucky and told them the deal wasn't going to work. This is a real testament to my dad's integrity to be transparent and honorable. Instead of pulling out of the deal right away, dad's contact at the state suggested they still try out the new formula before pulling the deal.

The bad news was that the new formula did not work. The deal was dead, and my dad was responsible for a one million dollar loan. Please remember, my dad was a coach and teacher at a small private college that didn't pay him a big salary and was not a businessman. He wasn't prepared for this kind of blow, especially right out of the gate. He had no money, and instead of picking himself up, brushing himself off, and trying to turn this devastating experience around, he wallowed in his sorrow.

My mom and dad felt like they lost respect from the members of the community, and being bankrupt devastated them both. My mother felt embarrassed, humiliated, broken-hearted, and became a recluse. I am certain that this horrible experience helped kill her at the age of 63. My dad had no business experience and felt he had no one to turn to for help. He didn't know how to get out of this shaky situation and merely wallowed in his misery until the day he died.

What happened to my dad and our family motivated me to get into the financial business. I determined that I would understand the ins and outs of business so well, so thoroughly, that even if I should make a mistake someday – even a mistake on the order of the one my father made – I would be knowledgeable enough to negotiate my way through it, learn from my mistake and rise above it. The truth is, I wanted to be knowledgeable enough to never get into the kind of situation my father found himself in. And I vowed never to wallow in mistakes, but instead to learn from them. As a young man, I decided to help other families avoid the kind of devastation that ours suffered.

When I graduated from college, I went into banking. I wanted to go where the money was. I learned how banks make money by analyzing mortgages, debts, and cash flow. I was so good at analyzing businesses that I was recruited by a local insurance company and joined their investments department as a trainee. I traveled around the country inspecting and analyzing the hotels they owned.

After some time, the president of the insurance company approached me and told me he wanted me to join his son, who was a lawyer with a master's degree in business taxation, to start something called a "financial planning" business. Back in 1982, financial planning was in its infancy. We formed the business and created our own very successful process. From the outset, we focused on helping family businesses and corporate executives look at the big picture, define their values, and accelerate cash flow and growth in the value of the business or personal assets while simultaneously de-risking their business and personal economic model.

Way back in 1984, I was introduced to a process that became the real game-changer for our business and the businesses we served. Just now, more businesses are starting to understand and embrace the process we've been using for 30+ years. The process involves teaching business owners and corporate executives how not only to just accumulate money but to focus more on cash flow. That's similar to how banks make money. Banks don't just acquire assets that sit without producing capital. They only invest in assets that produce cash flow.

I use an analogy with my clients to explain the components of a vehicle compared to a business vehicle. Imagine building a vehicle with the following characteristics: it has a dune buggy body, a 100-gallon gas tank lined in lead, and a 2-cycle lawnmower engine. It has a lot of safe storage, but it won't be fast, nor will it be safe or comfortable should it rain, snow, or get in the path of high winds. So, you go back to the drawing table and redesign this vehicle with a semi-truck body, a 2-gallon gas tank, and a turbine engine. It has a lot of protection and a very fast potential start, but it won't go very far unless we constantly stop and fill it up with more fuel.

Now think about the vehicle you're driving now... it's got protection (i.e., seat belts, airbags, side collision bars, headrests, mirrors, etc.), a secure gas tank, comfortable interior, state-of-the-art technology, and a reliable engine.

Here is the "trick" question. What's the most important part of any vehicle?

Some of you may say the engine, some of you may say the gas tank, and some of you may say the protection part. These are all partially correct, but the best answer is the driver... YOU! Without you steering, braking, slowing down, speeding up, avoiding the chuckholes, gliding around the corners, going in the right direction, filling up the gas tank, checking the lights on the dashboard for mechanical issues, turning on or off the radio, not texting, adjusting the temperature, testing the tire pressure, etc.,

etc., etc., the vehicle will crash and burn before you reach the intended destination.

So, going back to business, what's the most important part of the business vehicle? Hopefully, you'll say that the people involved are what makes the business move forward in an accelerating mode based on your core values.

So WHY are you driving this vehicle compared to the myriad of other choices or options available? The answer is: it depends... and it solely depends... on YOU. With business owners or corporate executives, you have a unique WHY! Your "WHY" is the big question!

- Why are you in business?
- Why did you decide on your industry?
- Why don't you do something different?
- Why are you continuing to do what you're doing?

These are all questions determining your "WHY."

Once your "WHY' is determined, then you move to the "WHAT" question.

○ What can you do?
○ What shouldn't you be doing?
○ What can other people do better than you?
○ What can you teach others?
○ What actions need to be taken right away?
○ What steps need to be put on hold, and for how long?

How you design or redesign your business vehicle should be based around the same idea as the vehicle analogy. I believe that you should design your business with the same three main components in mind...

1) maximum protection
2) peace of mind savings
3) an efficient/effective business engine

These provide efficient cash flow that will lead to accelerated growth. This is a proven path to maximize your life's journey and leave a positive, long-standing legacy.

Over the years, I've met more business owners who were so focused on the day-to-day struggles in their businesses that they were not focused on the long-term business or personal objectives. I call that being focused "*in* the business, not *on* the business." It's a habit that any business can develop with the endless challenges that come up virtually on a daily basis. And when a business owner is focused on the business, typically, everyone else is agreeable with the direction.

A great example of this comes from my wife's family. Her grandfather had a very successful oil tooling business. It was very successful. He traveled around the world consulting and selling products. Then, he suddenly died of a heart attack at 61. He didn't have a succession plan. His son and son-in-law took over the business. It was very difficult to have a unified plan going forward. Family dynamics played a huge role. The missing patriarch left such a huge leadership hole that the business had to be sold.

Business owners must have a vision and keep that vision alive in their hearts and minds. And along with the vision is the very important motivation to provide incredible and differentiating value for your customers, teammates, and family. The reason why becomes very apparent. Knowing why you designed the business you did and why you are heading in a particular direction is very important. As the owner of your company, you can set your own targets and standards. And while the freedom of not having anyone standing in your way can be invigorating, the stress of knowing there is no one to blame for any failures can be too much to bear. This is when your "why" becomes imperative.

Everyone has a different reason for starting a business, but if that reason isn't compelling or if the owner loses sight of it, they may end up sharing the driving with someone who wants to go in a totally different direction. Before you know it, you look out the window, and you're headed to the desert instead of the ocean.

Creating a business is not that different to designing a vehicle that will serve the purpose of getting where you want to go, able to negotiate potholes that present themselves on the road of life, and getting the people who are traveling in the vehicle with you to the desired destination. And, very importantly, it helps to make sure the people you let into your vehicle want to go where you're headed as well.

Focusing *on* the business requires defining what you want your business to be in the long term and WHY. WHY requires defining your values. It requires making sure the entire team is on board and shares your values and visions. It requires making sure your family is on board. Is it just a business to give you something to do? Or is it a *family* business, a legacy you would like to exist long after you're gone by generating jobs and stability in your family for generations to come?

There are many potholes and roadblocks in life that affect businesses negatively. Our team refers to them as the 5 "D's":

- Divorce
- Disability
- Death
- Distress
- Disagreement

These are the events that we keep in mind as you de-risk your business. What would happen if…? We explore each of the scenarios and begin to build a strategy and a plan that will keep the business humming along should any of these disruptive "D's" come to pass.

Often, when any one of these events occurs, a business owner may be forced to sell. However, in order to get a business ready to sell takes time. You don't just put a "For Sale" sign on a business. If you are selling your home, you have to make it attractive and affordable for buyers, and that takes time and money. This is the same for all businesses. Are you sure the price you're asking is marketable? What's the potential current value of your business? Do you know how to improve the value? Do you know which parts of your business need improvement? We use a very effective process to help determine a range of values for your business, and what areas in your operations need improvement, if any. We also can show a business owner and their team how to determine which area or areas will take a lot of money or time to improve or abandon.

The Exit Planning Institute study shows that over 75% of business owners regret selling their business a year after selling their business. When business owners focus on how they will transition away from their business, their perspective shifts immediately. Focusing on a transition strategy involves more than what is right in front of the business owner at the moment. They have to be willing to invest the time and money required, and most importantly, they may have to be willing to change their thinking and their behavior. They will need to find a new purpose, direction, and significance.

I have learned that the "change" part of the equation is the hardest for most business owners. They may want things to be changed, however, they may not be ready to change. And it's not just the business owner who has to be open to change. Change has to be accepted by all involved in the organization's "wheel." Top-down thinking is 'old school,' and it rarely works when the owners start dictating the direction if everyone else is not aligned. I've seen more successful transitions occur when the business owner's vision for the business is seen as the hub of the entity. The spokes of the wheel involve the operations, accounting, marketing, logistics, human relations, vendors, and customer experience. If any of these spokes are dominant or minimized, the business wheel will see some pretty bumpy rides. It should be the passion of the business owner to make this ride as smooth as possible by developing, encouraging, and motivating all involved.

My passion is on improving cash flow, de-risking, and helping family businesses make a smooth transition when it's time to exit a business. While my life path was inspired by an event that left our family embarrassed and devastated, I use that experience to motivate me to learn how to help other families avoid having to go through anything like we went through. I have helped so many family businesses that were teetering on the brink of disaster. I've helped them change from scarcity thinking to an abundance mindset. I've helped them focus on their values and build their business on those values.

This life has provided treasures I could never have imagined for myself, my family, my staff, and my clients. I feel a great sense of joy and accomplishment every time I work with a business owner or corporate executive who is ready and willing to change and take decisive action. Watching individuals become focused on positive values, seeing them make that shift as their businesses get stronger and more successful based on a sturdy, unshakable foundation is priceless. I knew I wanted to learn from my dad's unfortunate experience. Fortunately, I have prevented misfortune from befalling so many others, and despite how their businesses may have started, they have ended up better than they could ever have imagined.

And that is a key thought: In business, how you end up is ultimately more important than how you start up.

Compliance approved: CRN202412-1445850

About Gary

Gary Woolman's work is to help family business owners "grow their enterprise and exit with a lasting purpose." He and his firm collaborate with other highly regarded specialists, specifically those who have years of experience working directly with business owners on accelerating the value of their businesses by focusing on both tangible and intangible factors. These experts' knowledge ranges from understanding financial performance to accelerating value through focusing on the 4 Cs: **Customer Capital**, **Human Capital**, **Structural Capital**, and **Social Capital**.

Gary's modest start in 1978 focused primarily on protection issues regarding death and/or disability of C-Suite executives and upper management in businesses in northeast Indiana. In 1981, Gary helped form Summit Consultants, Inc. in Fort Wayne, IN, as a fee-only financial planning firm. He stepped away from this business in 1984 to start a new venture, Woolman Financial Group, specializing in transition income planning for family business owners in the manufacturing sector and corporate executives in the auto and orthopedic industries. In 2002, Gary graduated from the Leadership Fort Wayne program, which provides leadership development to a diverse group of citizens to empower them to effectively serve their community.

Gary believes that "every day you should learn something new." This belief is evidenced by his hunger for knowledge and implementation of what he's learned. In 2016, he earned his Certified Family Business Specialist degree from the American College for Financial Services, and in 2021 he earned his Certified Exit Planning Advisor certification from the Exit Planning Institute.

His passion for working with the business owner segment was driven by two different business owner's stories, one who passed away suddenly and didn't prepare for this tragedy, and the second was a great story of how to successfully pass on their values for a lasting legacy.

Gary and his team successfully establish the core values of the business so that when, not if, the owners or key employees step away from the day-to-day operations, they can maintain their lifestyles for the rest of their lives and leave a sizable legacy to those they care about and love.

Outside of work, Gary and his wife Becky are deeply involved in their church life, where he has served as an Elder and currently as a Deacon in the Celebrate Recovery ministry. He also served on the board of The Discipleship Walk.

Gary is a proud father of two and the grandfather of six children. He loves to travel and spend time with the love of his life, Becky. Gary and Becky reside in Fort Wayne, Indiana.

Compliance approved: CRN202412-1445850

CPSIA information can be obtained
at www.ICGtesting.com
Printed in the USA
LVHW081503030522
717852LV00013B/274/J

9 781736 988145